SEC
FOOTBALL
TRIVIA

REVISED EDITION

SEC FOOTBALL TRIVIA

REVISED EDITION

COMPILED

BY

ERNIE COUCH

Rutledge Hill Press®
Nashville, Tennessee
A Thomas Nelson Company

Originally published as The Original SEC Tailgate Trivia.

Published by Rutledge Hill Press, a Thomas Nelson company, P.O. Box 141000 Nashville,
Tennessee 37214.

Library of Congress Cataloging-in-Publication Data

Couch, Ernie, 1949–
   SEC football trivia / compiled by Ernie Couch.—Rev. ed.
     p. cm.
   ISBN 1-55853-929-8 (pbk.)
    1. Southeastern Conference—Miscellanea. 2. Football—Southern States—Miscellanea. I. Title.
GV958.5.S59 C69 2001
796.332'63'0975—dc21

                                                    2001002042

Printed in the United States of America
01 02 03 04 05 — 5 4 3 2 1

PREFACE

Through the years the Southeastern Conference has produced some of the nation's most exciting college football. Volumes could be written on the fascinating players, coaches, and gridiron events of each of the SEC member schools. Captured within these pages are some of the highlights of this rich football heritage.

SEC Football Trivia is designed to be informative, educational, and entertaining. But most of all I hope that you will be motivated to learn more about the great football teams which comprise the Southeastern Conference.

Ernie Couch

TO

ROGER ABRAMSON

AND

THE GREAT SEC FOOTBALL FANS

TABLE OF CONTENTS

ALABAMA

CHAPTER ONE

When Alabama was admitted to the Union in 1819, the federal government authorized the state to set aside two townships in which to establish a "seminary of learning." In 1827 Tuscaloosa, then the state's capital, was chosen as the location for Alabama's first university.

On April 18, 1831, the University of Alabama opened with an enrollment of fifty-two students. The campus was comprised of seven buildings: two dorms, two faculty houses, a lab, a hotel (now Gorgas House), and the Rotunda. By 1841 the enrollment had jumped to sixty-three and the president's mansion was completed (its first occupant was University President Basil Manly). The 1850s saw the first fraternity opening on campus and the establishment of a medical college branch in Mobile.

In 1860 the University of Alabama became a military university with campus life conducted under a strict military discipline. During the Civil War the university helped provide quality leaders for the Confederate Army. In 1865 ten of the university's fourteen buildings were burned by Union troops. In the decade following the Civil War, the School of Law opened, and the early 1880s brought the establishment of the College of Engineering, the third oldest program of its type in the nation.

The 1890s were innovative times for the university. Its first football team hit the field. Its first woman student, Julia S.

ALABAMA

Tutwiler, enrolled, and the first student newspaper, the *Crimson-White*, hit the stands.

The University of Alabama entered the twentieth century with an enrollment of less than 400 students; it grew to over 5,000 by 1950. Enrollment sky rocketed through the last half of the twentieth century, and today the University of Alabama's twelve colleges and schools offer over 200 degree programs with a broad range of nationally recognized research programs and continuing educational opportunities.

Bryant-Denny Stadium

Q. In what year did the Crimson Tide play in its first bowl game?

A. 1926.

———————— 🏈 ————————

Q. In the 1990 matchup between Alabama and LSU, what Crimson Tide kicker posted six field goals?

A. Philip Doyle.

———————— 🏈 ————————

Q. How many seasons did Ray Perkins serve as head football coach at Alabama?

A. Four.

———————— 🏈 ————————

Q. What caused a lengthy delay during the 1995 Citrus Bowl in which Alabama beat Ohio State?

A. A stray dog on the field.

———————— 🏈 ————————

Q. What cub reporter covered the Tide practice sessions in Pasadena prior to the January 1, 1935, Rose Bowl contest?

A. Ronald Reagan.

———————— 🏈 ————————

Q. What three Alabama players were named in 1961 to All-American teams, the Tide's first since 1950?

A. Lee Roy Jordan, Pat Trammell, and Billy Neighbors.

———————— 🏈 ————————

Q. Who did Alabama defeat in the 1985 Aloha Bowl?

A. Southern California (24–3).

Q. What great back for Alabama in the 1920s went on to become a famous cowboy movie star?

A. Johnny Mack Brown.

Q. Where did lefthanded passer Mike Shula rank nationwide in passing efficiency in 1958?

A. Fifth.

Q. What was the final score of Alabama's first game, played against Professor Taylor's school and Birmingham high school students?

A. 56–0.

Q. What *Birmingham News* sports reporter popularized Alabama's nickname, Crimson Tide?

A. Zipp Newman.

Q. With what season record did Coach Bill Curry lead the Tide to being named the 1989 SEC Champions?

A. 10–2.

Q. During what years did Paul "Bear" Bryant play for the Crimson Tide?

A. 1933, 1934, and 1935.

Q. Ozzie Newsome joined what professional team in 1978?

A. Cleveland Browns.

Q. In what year was the 16,000 square-foot Paul W. Bryant Museum opened?

A. 1988.

———————— 🏈 ————————

Q. The Billy Neighbors Most Improved Defensive Lineman Award was given to what 1983 defensive tackle?

A. Jon Hand.

———————— 🏈 ————————

Q. In addition to tying two school records in kicking and scoring, how many school records did Van Tiffin set at the completion of his senior year?

A. Nine.

———————— 🏈 ————————

Q. In what year did the Crimson Tide record its first perfect season, including a bowl game?

A. 1925.

———————— 🏈 ————————

Q. Who held the record for most rushes in a season prior to Shaun Alexander's 1999 record of 302?

A. Sherman Williams (291).

———————— 🏈 ————————

Q. A team record for most points scored in a bowl game (61 against Syracuse) was set in what 1953 bowl?

A. Orange Bowl.

———————— 🏈 ————————

Q. Who brought football to Alabama, earning himself recognition as the father of University of Alabama football?

A. W. G. Little.

Q. Between 1945 and 1993 Alabama secured how many Sugar Bowl victories?

A. Twelve.

––––––––––––– 🏈 –––––––––––––

Q. What was the 1986 Crimson Tide record?

A. 10–3.

––––––––––––– 🏈 –––––––––––––

Q. Alabama played and won its first night game in what year?

A. 1940.

––––––––––––– 🏈 –––––––––––––

Q. Who set a new Alabama record during the 1986 season for most yards gained in one game?

A. Bobby Humphrey (284 yards).

––––––––––––– 🏈 –––––––––––––

Q. Who was the second Alabama player named an All-American?

A. Pooley Hubert.

––––––––––––– 🏈 –––––––––––––

Q. In what year did Alabama and Auburn resume playing each other after a forty-year dispute?

A. 1948.

––––––––––––– 🏈 –––––––––––––

Q. During the first twenty years of football at Alabama, how many different individuals served as coach?

A. Twelve.

Q. Rudy Vallee composed the song "Football Freddie" and dedicated it to what Crimson Tide lineman?

A. Fred Sington.

———— 🏈 ————

Q. What was Alabama's 1992 record?

A. 13–0.

———— 🏈 ————

Q. What Crimson Tide All-American of the early 1930s later was an assistant coach at Ole Miss?

A. Johnny Cain.

———— 🏈 ————

Q. What record margin of victory for a Liberty Bowl game did Alabama set in 1976?

A. Thirty (Alabama 36—UCLA 6).

———— 🏈 ————

Q. Wallace Wade served as assistant coach at what university before taking the head post at Alabama?

A. Vanderbilt.

———— 🏈 ————

Q. What former 1938–39 Tidesman became internationally known as a blind golfer?

A. Charley Boswell.

———— 🏈 ————

Q. What was the total number of consecutive victories Alabama posted during the Tide's great 1991–93 winning streak?

A. Twenty-eight.

Q. Bart Starr played quarterback on the 1955 team under what head coach?

A. J. B. Whitworth.

Q. What is the name of Alabama's home playing field in Birmingham?

A. Legion Field.

Q. What Crimson Tide linebacker was named recipient of the prestigious Vince Lombardi Award in 1986?

A. Cornelius Bennett.

Q. In the New Year's Day FedEx 2000 Orange Bowl, what team defeated Alabama by one point?

A. Michigan (35–34).

Q. In the 1935 Rose Bowl, who set the Alabama individual bowl game record for longest run from scrimmage?

A. Dixie Howell (67 yards).

Q. Under what coach did the Tide gain its first national recognition?

A. Xen Scott.

Q. Who quarterbacked the 1968, 1969, and 1970 Alabama teams?

A. Scott Hunter.

Q. What term did sportswriters use to describe Alabama's linemen in 1930, leading to the adoption of the elephant mascot?

A. "Red Elephants."

Q. Big John Hannah signed with what NFL team in 1973?

A. New England Patriots.

Q. Alabama All-American tackle W. T. VandeGraaf (1915) was known by what nickname?

A. "Bully."

Q. Who received the 1986 Ray Perkins Most Improved Receiver Award?

A. Greg Payne, flanker.

Q. Joe Namath missed quarterbacking in what bowl contest because he was suspended?

A. 1964 Sugar Bowl.

Q. In the United Press International (UPI) rankings, which were issued from 1950 through 1996, how many times was Alabama ranked No. 1?

A. Five.

Q. Steve Sloan followed his Alabama career by quarterbacking for what NFL team?

A. Atlanta Falcons.

Q. What Tidesman made the longest punt of the 1986 SEC season, a 73-yarder against Notre Dame?

A. Chris Mohr.

———— 🏈 ————

Q. What Tide halfback was the first player to score touchdowns in four consecutive bowl games?

A. Major Ogilvie.

———— 🏈 ————

Q. At the hands of what team did Alabama suffer a 38–7 defeat in the 1999 Music City Bowl?

A. Virginia Tech.

———— 🏈 ————

Q. Alabama defeated what team 20–19 in its first bowl game?

A. University of Washington Huskies.

———— 🏈 ————

Q. What Alabama senior ended the 1986 season as all-time scoring leader?

A. Van Tiffin (312 points).

———— 🏈 ————

Q. On October 20, 1951, Alabama played its first television game against what competitor?

A. Tennessee.

———— 🏈 ————

Q. What defensive Tidesmen were named to the UPI All-SEC team in 1985 and 1986?

A. Curt Jarvis and Cornelius Bennett.

Q. Ending his days at Alabama, Joe Namath signed a contract with which NFL team for $400,000?

A. New York Jets.

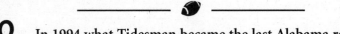

Q. In 1994 what Tidesman became the last Alabama recipient of the *Nashville Banner* Award?

A. Jay Baker.

Q. What Alabama wide receiver was selected to play in the 1987 Japan Bowl and Senior Bowl?

A. Albert Bell.

Q. What is the name of the Alabama mascot?

A. "Big Al."

Q. In 1979 what Alabama linebacker was named Outstading Player of the Sugar Bowl?

A. Barry Krauss.

Q. In what years did "Bear" Bryant receive National Coach of the Year awards?

A. 1961, 1971, and 1973.

Q. By what nickname was quarterback Ken Stabler known?

A. "Snake."

ALABAMA

Q. What one-handed line coach came to Alabama under head coach Xen Scott in 1921 and enjoyed a more than forty-year career at the Capstone?

A. Hank Crisp.

————— 🏈 —————

Q. The Outstanding Player Award for defensive play in the 1970 Astro-Bluebonnet Bowl went to what Tide linebacker?

A. Jeff Rouzie.

————— 🏈 —————

Q. What former Tidesman was the sixth round 1986 draft choice of the Dallas Cowboys?

A. Thornton Chandler.

————— 🏈 —————

Q. Alabama rolled to a 17–4 victory over what team in the 1997 Outback Bowl?

A. Michigan.

————— 🏈 —————

Q. For how many years did Mike DuBose serve as an assistant coach prior to being named head football coach at Alabama on December 9, 1996?

A. Twenty-one years.

————— 🏈 —————

Q. What junior was Alabama's second leading tackler in 1985?

A. Joe Godwin.

————— 🏈 —————

Q. How many times during the twentieth century was Alabama honored as SEC Football Champion?

A. Twenty-one.

Q. Following the 1986 season, Coach Ray Perkins accepted the head coach position and vice president of what NFL team?

A. Tampa Bay Buccaneers.

Q. Alabama's come-from-behind second-half rally led to a 30–25 win over what opponent in the 1991 Blockbuster Bowl?

A. Colorado.

Q. What halfback was named Outstanding Offensive Player of the 1985 Aloha Bowl?

A. Gene Jelks.

Q. The Tide handed what No. 1-ranked team a 34–13 defeat in the 1993 Sugar Bowl?

A. Miami.

Q. In the 1926 Rose Bowl what back received the Outstanding Player Award?

A. Johnny Mack Brown.

Q. What junior linebacker had 18 quarterback sacks and two blocked punts for Alabama during the 1987 season?

A. Derrick Thomas.

Q. In what year did Alabama play its first football game?

A. 1892.

Q. What three All-Americans played in the 1934 Rose Bowl for Alabama?

A. Bill Lee, Don Hutson, and Dixie Howell.

———————— 🏈 ————————

Q. What Tider went on to lead the NFL in scoring five times while a member of the Green Bay Packers?

A. Don Hutson.

———————— 🏈 ————————

Q. During the 1954 Cotton Bowl, what overzealous Tidesman lunged from the Alabama bench and tackled the Rice runner at midfield?

A. Tommy Lewis.

———————— 🏈 ————————

Q. What former Tidesman was named 1985 NFL Man of the Year?

A. Dwight Stephenson of the Miami Dolphins.

———————— 🏈 ————————

Q. What coach succeeded Wallace Wade as head mentor in 1931?

A. Frank Thomas.

———————— 🏈 ————————

Q. Alabama scored 56 points in one game against which team during the 1986 season?

A. Tennessee.

———————— 🏈 ————————

Q. Paul "Bear" Bryant participated in which bowl game as a player?

A. 1934 Rose Bowl.

Q. What center anchored the 1986 Alabama offensive line?

A. Wes Neighbors.

Q. What year did Alabama play its first Southern Conference game?

A. 1895.

Q. Lee Roy Jordan played for what NFL team?

A. Dallas Cowboys.

Q. In what bowl did Alabama defeat Nebraska 34–7?

A. 1967 Sugar Bowl.

Q. What coach took the Tide to its first SEC Championship?

A. Frank Thomas.

Q. What Alabama quarterback received Academic All-Southeastern Conference honors in 1981 and 1983?

A. Walter Lewis.

Q. Due to his show business interests, what nickname was given to Joe Namath?

A. "Broadway Joe."

ALABAMA

Q. How many times did Alabama meet Stanford in the Rose Bowl?

A. Twice: 1927 and 1935.

———— 🏈 ————

Q. Following his collegiate career at Alabama, Johnny Musso played for what NFL team from 1975 to 1977?

A. Chicago Bears.

———— 🏈 ————

Q. "Bear" Bryant took his teams to how many straight bowl appearances?

A. Twenty-four.

———— 🏈 ————

Q. What Tidesman won the Jerry Duncan I Like To Practice Award in 1984?

A. Randy Rockwell, linebacker.

———— 🏈 ————

Q. Bart Starr is a native of what city?

A. Montgomery.

———— 🏈 ————

Q. Which two Crimson Tide players each posted ten pass breakups in 1990?

A. Stacy Harrison and Mark McMillian.

———— 🏈 ————

Q. Alabama scored its first perfect season in 1897 with what record?

A. 1–0–0.

ALABAMA

Q. Who was the only Alabama player chosen All-American under Coach Red Drew?

A. Ed Salem.

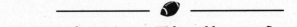

Q. In 2000 what Crimson Tide tackle was a first-round draft pick of the Washington Redskins?

A. Chris Samuels.

Q. What Tide linebacker played for the New York Jets from 1966 to 1974?

A. Paul Crane.

Q. Fearing Alabama's speed, what type of special equipment did coach "Pop" Warner of Stanford issue to his players for the 1927 Rose Bowl?

A. Lightweight silk pants.

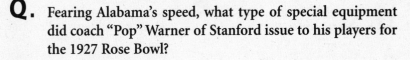

Q. In what year did Paul W. Bryant come to Alabama as head coach?

A. 1958.

Q. In 1945 what Tide halfback was voted the SEC's Most Valuable Player over Georgia's Charley Trippi?

A. Harry Gilmer.

Q. What Alabama All-American became the school's all-time leading rusher in 1987?

A. Bobby Humphrey.

ALABAMA

Q. What former Crimson Tide player served as the team physician from 1959 until 1971?

A. Dr. Bill Baty.

Q. In 1999 who became the sixth Crimson Tide player to be inducted into the Pro Football Hall of Fame?

A. Ozzie Newsome.

Q. Who coached the Tide to its first bowl victory?

A. Wallace Wade.

Q. What Alabama cornerback earned first-team All-SEC honors in 1998?

A. Fernando Bryant.

Q. What Crimson Tide team allowed the fewest yards for an entire season?

A. 1938 (596 yards).

Q. Who received the 1965 Orange Bowl Outstanding Player Award?

A. Joe Namath.

Q. In the 1968 Gator Bowl, Alabama set a team bowl game record by allowing Missouri how many yards passing?

A. None.

Q. During the 1992 season what Tide player racked up 21.5 sacks?

A. John Copeland.

———————— 🏈 ————————

Q. The efforts of what famous passing-receiving duo brought victory to Alabama in the 1934 Rose Bowl?

A. Dixie Howell and Don Hutson.

———————— 🏈 ————————

Q. In what year did coach Frank Thomas make Paul "Bear" Bryant a coaching assistant at Alabama?

A. 1936.

———————— 🏈 ————————

Q. In the back-to-back seasons of 1989 and 1990 what Tidesman received All-SEC honors?

A. Terrill Chatman.

———————— 🏈 ————————

Q. Who was named Most Valuable Player of the 1986 Sun Bowl?

A. Cornelius Bennett.

———————— 🏈 ————————

Q. Frank Thomas hired which three assistants who later would be head coaches at Tuscaloosa?

A. Red Drew, J. B. Whitworth, and "Bear" Bryant.

———————— 🏈 ————————

Q. In the 1988 Sun Bowl, what quarterback set the Alabama individual bowl game record for most yards passing?

A. David Smith (412 yards).

Q. In what bowl game did center Wes Neighbors receive the Most Outstanding Lineman Award?

A. 1983 Sun Bowl.

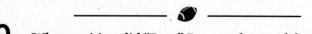

Q. What position did "Bear" Bryant play at Alabama?

A. End.

Q. Alabama was chosen to play what team in the 1986 Kickoff Classic?

A. Ohio State.

Q. What quarterback ended his regular season career by setting a record with thirty-five touchdown passes?

A. Mike Shula.

Q. What 1938 Alabama All-American eventually gained more fame as a professional wrestler?

A. Arthur "Tarzan" White.

Q. What team did Coach Frank Thomas refer to as his "War Babies"?

A. The 1944 team, which was basically comprised of freshmen.

Q. In what bowl game was Alabama penalized eighteen times, setting a bowl game team record?

A. 2000 Orange Bowl.

ALABAMA

Q. Who is the current play-by-play "voice of the Crimson Tide"?

A. Paul Kennedy.

_____ 🏈 _____

Q. During the 1986 season a team record was set for how many rushing first downs in a single game?

A. Twenty-eight (against Mississippi State).

_____ 🏈 _____

Q. In both 1993 and 1994, what Alabama placekicker was named All-American?

A. Michael Proctor.

_____ 🏈 _____

Q. Who was selected as head football coach of Alabama on January 4, 1987?

A. Bill Curry.

_____ 🏈 _____

Q. What year was Ray Perkins redshirted?

A. 1963.

_____ 🏈 _____

Q. When did the Crimson Tide make an appearance in the Sun Bowl prior to 1986?

A. 1983 (Alabama vs. SMU).

_____ 🏈 _____

Q. During his 1990–96 seasons as Alabama's head football coach, Gene Stallings led the Tide to what win/loss record?

A. 62–25–0.

ALABAMA

Q. What Alabama team scored the most points in one season?

A. 1973 (454 points).

———————— 🏈 ————————

Q. For five years Ray Perkins was a receiver for what professional team?

A. Baltimore Colts.

———————— 🏈 ————————

Q. In what year did the Tide play its first television game in Tuscaloosa?

A. 1979.

———————— 🏈 ————————

Q. What former Tide quarterback was chosen athletic director in 1987?

A. Steve Sloan.

———————— 🏈 ————————

Q. During his 1989–90 career at Alabama, Gary Hollingsworth averaged how many yards per game?

A. 170.9.

———————— 🏈 ————————

Q. Ray Ogden's 108-yard kickoff return in 1964 was against what Crimson Tide foe?

A. Auburn.

———————— 🏈 ————————

Q. On January 31, 1999, what former four-year letterman at Alabama played in Super Bowl XXXIII?

A. Curtis Alexander (Denver Broncos).

ARKANSAS

CHAPTER TWO

The University of Arkansas is situated in the heart of the beautiful Ozark Mountains in the northwest portion of the state. Established under the provisions of the Morrell Act in 1871 as both the state university and the land-grant college of Arkansas, the university opened its doors in Fayetteville to students on January 22, 1872. The location was determined by statewide elections that were held for the purpose of voting bond issues, or subscriptions, to establish the university. Washington County and the city of Fayetteville placed a winning bid of $130,000 with the state appropriating an additional $50,000. The 160-acre homestead of William McIlroy was purchased to serve as the campus.

The McIlroy home was remodeled for classroom space, and a small two-story frame building was constructed for additional classes. The enrollment on opening day was eight students with three faculty members. In 1875 construction was completed on Old Main, which has become known nationally as "the symbol of higher education in Arkansas." Today Old Main is home to the Fulbright College of Arts and Sciences, with its five academic departments and honors program.

The university's campus includes over 170 buildings situated on 337 acres. One truly unique aspect of the University of Arkansas campus is the Senior Walk, which winds around the campus for a length of almost five miles. This sidewalk has the name of every graduate, dating back to the class of 1876, etched into its concrete surface.

The University of Arkansas offers over 200 undergraduate and graduate degrees in more than 150 fields of study. The academic divisions on the Fayetteville campus include eight colleges and schools. From the humble beginnings of the early 1870s, the university has grown into one of the leading institutes of higher learning in the southeastern United States and a powerhouse in collegiate athletics.

Donald W. Reynolds
Razorback Stadium

Courtesy of University of Arkansas Sports Information Department

Q. In the 1995 matchup with South Carolina, which Razorback scored an incredible six touchdowns?

A. Madre Hill.

————————— 🏈 —————————

Q. In 1922 who was selected as the first Razorback Homecoming Queen?

A. Aliece McHenry.

————————— 🏈 —————————

Q. Coach Frank Broyles made his bowl debut as Arkansas head coach leading the Razorbacks to a 14–7 win over what school in the 1960 Gator Bowl?

A. Georgia Tech.

————————— 🏈 —————————

Q. Arkansas's early football teams were known by what name?

A. Cardinals.

————————— 🏈 —————————

Q. In 1938 who became the first Razorback designated as a first-round draft pick by a professional team?

A. Jack Robbins (Chicago Cardinals).

————————— 🏈 —————————

Q. Two games of the Arkansas Industrial University's 1894 three-game season were against a team representing what school?

A. Fort Smith High School.

————————— 🏈 —————————

Q. What spacious facility that opened on the University of Arkansas campus in 1998 serves as the Razorback football practice area in inclement weather?

A. The Willard and Pat Walker Pavilion.

Q. The Razorbacks rolled over what team in the 1911 season opener?

A. Southwest Missouri (100–0).

———————— 🏈 ————————

Q. What young Latin instructor and later University of Arkansas president volunteered to serve as Arkansas's first football coach?

A. John C. Futrall.

———————— 🏈 ————————

Q. The expansion and renovation work at Donald W. Reynolds Razorback Stadium for the 2001 season increased the fan seating to what number?

A. 72,000.

———————— 🏈 ————————

Q. Who is the only Razorback to have earned a master's degree prior to having played in his final collegiate game?

A. Brandon Burlsworth.

———————— 🏈 ————————

Q. From 1947 to 2000 Arkansas played in how many Cotton Bowl Games?

A. Nine.

———————— 🏈 ————————

Q. Who served as Arkansas's first quarterback on the 1894 squad?

A. Wright Lindsey.

———————— 🏈 ————————

Q. In what year did the Razorbacks first utilize air travel to and from away games?

A. 1946.

Q. The father of which Arkansas head football coach served many years as the athletic director and head basketball coach at the Arkansas School for the Deaf in Little Rock?

A. Houston Nutt.

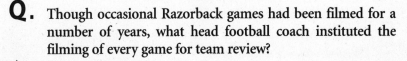

Q. Though occasional Razorback games had been filmed for a number of years, what head football coach instituted the filming of every game for team review?

A. John Barnhill.

Q. In the 1969 35th Sugar Bowl Classic, who did Arkansas defeat 16–2?

A. Georgia.

Q. Who did Arkansas hire as head football coach in 1908?

A. Hugo Bezdek.

Q. The 1970 Sugar Bowl saw Arkansas fall victim to what school?

A. Mississippi (27–22).

Q. In 1898 what three-time captain for Arkansas died from complications of a cold contracted on a football outing to Springfield, Missouri?

A. Herbert Fishback.

Q. During the 1901 matchup with a Little Rock athletic club, what UA coach actually played part of the game when injuries left the Arkansas team shorthanded?

A. Coach Charlie Thomas.

Q. What two Razorback 1970s-era quarterbacks were selected by the *Texas/Arkansas Football* Magazine as Southwest Conference Outstanding Player of the Year and received the Dana X. Bible Award?

A. Scott Bull (1975) and Kevin Scanlon (1979).

Q. Award-winning 1920s Razorback Garland Beavers was known by what nickname?

A. "Bevo."

Q. Who lost to Arkansas 34–15 in the 1980 Hall of Fame Bowl?

A. Tulane.

Q. On January 1, 1934, in the Dixie Classic, a forerunner of the Cotton Bowl, Arkansas tied what opponent?

A. Centenary (7–7).

Q. In what year did Razorback Dick Bumpas receive All-American honors?

A. 1970.

Q. Who fell prey to Arkansas in the 1971 Liberty Bowl?

A. Tennessee (14–13).

Q. How many field goals did Kendall Trainor make in 1988, setting a Razorback record for most consecutive field goals made in a season?

A. Twenty-four.

Q. At 5–0 who was the only school to defeat Arkansas during the 1910 season?

A. Kansas State.

———————— 🏈 ————————

Q. Which 1930s Arkansas passer was known as "Paddlefoot?"

A. Dwight Sloan.

———————— 🏈 ————————

Q. In what year did Arkansas secure its first official Southwest Conference title?

A. 1936.

———————— 🏈 ————————

Q. In 1923 the Razorbacks set a school record by posting how many shutouts against opponents?

A. Six.

———————— 🏈 ————————

Q. With how many plays did Arkansas set a school record for most plays in a single game when facing Wichita State University in 1969?

A. 110.

———————— 🏈 ————————

Q. In the 1975 game against Air Force, how many penalties did Arkansas receive, setting a new school record?

A. Seventeen.

———————— 🏈 ————————

Q. Glen Rose, who served as Razorback head football coach during the 1944–45 seasons, was born near what Tennessee town?

A. Savannah.

Q. In the 1981 Gator Bowl that was played in fog, Arkansas was defeated 31–27 by what opponent?

A. North Carolina.

———————— 🏈 ————————

Q. With how many points did Arkansas tie Rice in 1971; Southern Methodist in 1974; and Auburn in 1992?

A. Twenty-four.

———————— 🏈 ————————

Q. During the 1963 Sugar Bowl, what players set a Razorback bowl record for longest pass completed?

A. Bill Gray to Jerry Lamb (68 yards).

———————— 🏈 ————————

Q. Who served as head football coach at Arkansas from 1977 to 1983?

A. Lou Holtz.

———————— 🏈 ————————

Q. What Arkansas football coach was said to have always slept with a pencil under his pillow so that he could jot down any new plays that might come to him in the night?

A. Francis Schmidt.

———————— 🏈 ————————

Q. The Fighting Razorback, uniformed mascot of Arkansas, has what two additional family members?

A. Sue E. and Pork Chop.

———————— 🏈 ————————

Q. Constructed as a WPA project, what was the seating capacity of Razorback Stadium when first opened for the 1938 season?

A. 13,500.

Q. On November 23, 1991, who did Arkansas shut out 20–0 in the last SWC game to be played at War Memorial Stadium in Little Rock?

A. Rice.

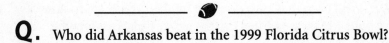

Q. Who did Arkansas beat in the 1999 Florida Citrus Bowl?

A. Michigan (45–31).

Q. Which Razorback coach started his collegiate coaching career at age 28 as head football coach at Wichita State University?

A. Jack Mitchell.

Q. During the 1999 Florida Citrus Bowl, who set a Razorback bowl record with 42 attempted passes?

A. Clint Stoerner.

Q. Making its debut at Razorback games in the 1960s, what was the name of Arkansas's live mascot?

A. Big Red I.

Q. In the summer of 1990, Arkansas announced its plan to affiliate with what intercollegiate sports conference?

A. Southeastern Conference (SEC).

Q. Who did the Razorbacks face and defeat 28–14 in the 1982 Bluebonnet Bowl?

A. Florida.

Q. In 1950 what Razorback was a first-round draft pick of the Cleveland Browns?

A. Preston Carpenter.

Q. Who served as interim head football coach at Arkansas for the 1943 season when Coach George Cole went into the Navy?

A. John "Bud" Tomlin.

Q. With just 21 seconds left in the 1985 Holiday Bowl, what freshman Razorback kicked a 37-yard field goal to clinch an 18–17 victory over Arizona State?

A. Kindall Trainor.

Q. In 1983 what two Razorbacks were first-round draft picks of the San Diego Chargers?

A. Gary Atwater and Billy Ray Smith Jr.

Q. What is the official Internet site of Razorback men's sports, including football?

A. www.hogwired.com.

Q. What player recognized as the state's first high school football star joined the Razorbacks as a freshman in 1910?

A. Russell May.

Q. On December 2, 1954, appreciative Razorback fans gave what gift to coach Bowden Wyatt in recognition of a stellar season, only to have him break contract the following week for a position at Tennessee?

A. A new Cadillac.

Q. What was Coach Francis Schmidt's (1922–28) record at Arkansas?

A. 42–20–3.

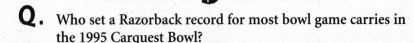

Q. Who set a Razorback record for most bowl game carries in the 1995 Carquest Bowl?

A. Marius Johnson (29 carries).

Q. To what multi-talented gridiron star was the 1920 University of Arkansas yearbook dedicated?

A. Gene "Sodie" Davidson.

Q. The decimation of most of the Razorback squad by military service led to a miserable 103–0 defeat at the hands of what team in 1918?

A. Oklahoma.

Q. Both Bruce Maxwell in the 1970 Sugar Bowl and Gary Anderson in the 1980 Hall of Fame Bowl set a Razorback bowl record for longest run from scrimmage with how many yards?

A. Forty-six.

Q. When opened in 1938 what name was temporarily given to the Razorback Stadium?

A. Bailey Stadium (for then-governor Carl E. Bailey).

Q. During the twentieth century what was the only recorded game in which Arkansas received zero penalties?

A. Texas A&M (1967).

ARKANSAS

Q. Over a 1905 officiating dispute, Arkansas severed athletic relations with what Missouri school for two seasons?

A. Rolla School of Mines.

Q. In 1914 Arkansas became a founding member of what intercollegiate sports organization?

A. Southwestern Intercollegiate Athletic Conference (SIAC).

Q. At the hands of what two schools did the Razorbacks suffer back-to-back Cotton Bowl defeats?

A. UCLA (1989) and Tennessee (1990).

Q. What Arkansas coach mortgaged his home and put the money into the Arkansas Loyalty League to help insure the existence of a Razorback team for the 1933 season?

A. Fred Thomsen.

Q. The ineligibility of which Razorback led the Southwest Conference to declare that no championship would be announced for the 1933 season?

A. Ulysses S. "Heinie" Schleuter.

Q. Historically listed as Arkansas's lightest team, what was the average weight of the 1917 Razorbacks?

A. 157 pounds.

Q. The Oklahoma Sooners decimated the Razorbacks racking up what final score in the 1987 Orange Bowl?

A. 42–8.

Q. In back-to-back Sugar Bowl games Arkansas suffered defeat at the hands of what two schools?

A. Alabama (1962) and Mississippi (1963).

———————— 🏈 ————————

Q. What early 1950s Razorback became the number one draft pick of the Chicago Cardinals?

A. Lamar McHan.

———————— 🏈 ————————

Q. In 1922 following a string of volunteers and part-timers, who became the first "regular" assistant football coach at Arkansas?

A. Ivan H. Grove.

———————— 🏈 ————————

Q. What former Pittsburgh 1917 All-American served as head football coach at Arkansas during the 1920–21 seasons?

A. George McLaren.

———————— 🏈 ————————

Q. How many seasons did Fred Thomsen serve as head football coach at Arkansas?

A. Thirteen.

———————— 🏈 ————————

Q. From his 1937 All-American season until 1963, Jim Benton held the SWC record for most catches in a season with how many receptions?

A. Forty-eight (814 yards).

———————— 🏈 ————————

Q. During the 1978 Orange Bowl, Roland Sales set a Razorback bowl record for most yards gained rushing against Oklahoma with how many yards?

A. 205.

Q. Where did Arkansas defeat LSU 16–0 on November 13, 1909?

A. Memphis, Tennessee.

———————— 🏈 ————————

Q. Who handed Arkansas a 24–9 defeat in the 1980 Cotton Bowl?

A. Alabama.

———————— 🏈 ————————

Q. What former Tennessee player, who had captained the 1938 Vols' 11–0 team, served as head football coach at Arkansas during the 1953 and 1954 seasons?

A. Bowden Wyatt.

———————— 🏈 ————————

Q. Where did John Barnhill coach prior to being called as head football coach and athletic director at Arkansas?

A. University of Tennessee.

———————— 🏈 ————————

Q. Who was the first three-time All-Southwest Conference Razorback?

A. Clyde L. Scott.

———————— 🏈 ————————

Q. To what school in the 1991 Independence Bowl did the Razorbacks lose 24–15?

A. Georgia.

———————— 🏈 ————————

Q. Who did the Razorbacks play to a scoreless tie in ice and snow at the Cotton Bowl in Dallas on New Year's Day 1947?

A. Louisiana State University.

Q. Due to a badly torn jersey (No. 23), what number did George Cole wear in the 1927 victory over Texas Christian prompting accusations of foul play?

A. Twenty-two.

———— 🏈 ————

Q. What was the first season the Razorbacks were ranked in the Top Ten nationally by The Associated Press and United Press International?

A. 1954.

———— 🏈 ————

Q. Where was the 1947 game between Texas and Arkansas moved to accommodate the large number of fans?

A. Crump Stadium, Memphis, Tennessee.

———— 🏈 ————

Q. What school defeated Arkansas by one point in the 1961 Cotton Bowl?

A. Duke (7–6).

———— 🏈 ————

Q. When was Arkansas's first perfect season?

A. 1909.

———— 🏈 ————

Q. What Big Eight Champion did Arkansas defeat 10–7 in the 1965 Cotton Bowl?

A. Nebraska.

———— 🏈 ————

Q. Who did the Razorbacks defeat 40–6 in the inaugural game at War Memorial Stadium in Little Rock on September 18, 1948?

A. Abilene Christian.

ARKANSAS

Q. Noted for his speed as a sprinter and hurdler in track, what Razorback of the late 1940s was billed as "the fastest man in college football?"

A. Clyde L. Scott.

———————— 🏈 ————————

Q. Who did Arkansas tie 10–10 in the 1978 Fiesta Bowl?

A. UCLA.

———————— 🏈 ————————

Q. Clyde L. Scott's retired jersey No. 12 was "un-retired" by what Arkansas kicker only to once again be retired following his college career?

A. Steve Little.

———————— 🏈 ————————

Q. A formal protest filed by the coach of what team led to the Razorbacks being officially censured by the Southwest Conference for "rough football" in 1949?

A. Texas Christian.

———————— 🏈 ————————

Q. What mid-twentieth century Razorback became a noted placekicker for the New York Giants and later a major television network sportscaster?

A. Pat Summerall.

———————— 🏈 ————————

Q. What three-year Arkansas letterman and Congressional Medal of Honor winner was the featured speaker at the dedication of War Memorial Stadium in Little Rock on September 18, 1948?

A. Maurice "Footsie" Britt.

———————— 🏈 ————————

Q. The 1954 season Razorback team was known by what title?

A. "The 25 Little Pigs."

ARKANSAS

Q. Having gone 68 games without achieving a shutout against an opponent, who did the Razorbacks beat 41–0 in 1954?

A. Tulsa.

———————— 🏈 ————————

Q. With 38,000 fans on hand, who did the Razorbacks defeat 6–0 in the first absolute "sell-out crowd" at War Memorial Stadium in Little Rock on October 23, 1954?

A. Mississippi.

———————— 🏈 ————————

Q. During the twentieth century who served the most seasons as head football coach at Arkansas?

A. Frank Broyles (19 seasons).

———————— 🏈 ————————

Q. What was the name given the wild hog captured by a Leola farmer that served as Arkansas's live animal mascot for the 1977 season?

A. Ragnar.

———————— 🏈 ————————

Q. In 1978 and again in 1987 Arkansas played in what bowl game?

A. Orange Bowl.

———————— 🏈 ————————

Q. Having first installed artificial turf in War Memorial Stadium for the 1970 season, what year did the facility return to a natural grass playing field?

A. 1994.

———————— 🏈 ————————

Q. Who is credited with coining the name "Razorbacks" for the Arkansas football team?

A. Coach Hugo Bezdek.

Q. With 18 interceptions, which Razorback holds the Arkansas record for intercepting the most passes in a season?

A. Kay Eakin (1939).

———————— 🏈 ————————

Q. Who did Arkansas defeat 39–0 in the first game played under lights at War Memorial Stadium on September 20, 1969?

A. Oklahoma State.

———————— 🏈 ————————

Q. To which school did Arkansas lose its first away game on Thanksgiving Day 1894?

A. University of Texas at Austin.

———————— 🏈 ————————

Q. The September 19, 1992, matchup between Arkansas and Alabama set a War Memorial attendance record for a Razorback game with how many people?

A. 55,912.

———————— 🏈 ————————

Q. In a come-from-behind win, Arkansas defeated what school in the 1948 Dixie Bowl?

A. William & Mary (21–19).

———————— 🏈 ————————

Q. During the 1960s who became the second Razorback to receive recognition as a three-time All-Southwest Conference honoree?

A. Loyd Phillips.

———————— 🏈 ————————

Q. Arkansas suffered its first postseason defeat to what opponent in the 1955 Cotton Bowl?

A. Georgia Tech (14–6).

Q. To how many bowl victories did Head Coach Lou Holtz lead the Razorbacks?

A. Three.

————  ————

Q. What was the only school to defeat Arkansas during the 1910 season?

A. Kansas State (5–0).

————  ————

Q. In the 1980 Sugar Bowl who set a Razorback bowl record with 22 passes completed?

A. Kevin Scanlon.

————  ————

Q. Following the 1998 season what Razorback All-American offensive guard's jersey was retired?

A. Brandon Burlsworth (No. 77).

————  ————

Q. In 1961 who became the first Razorback to represent Arkansas in the Hula Bowl?

A. Halfback Lance Alworth.

————  ————

Q. During the 1913 season what Arkansas freshman quarterback was persuaded to transfer to Quachita Baptist College?

A. J. L. "Nick" Carter.

————  ————

Q. What record number of Razorbacks represented Arkansas in the 1999 postseason Senior Bowl in Mobile, Alabama?

A. Five.

Q. In 1982 which Razorback became the first recipient of the Steve Little Award?

A. Keith Burns.

Q. In what season did Arkansas play only one game?

A. 1895.

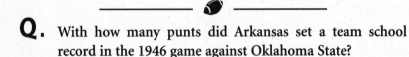

Q. With how many punts did Arkansas set a team school record in the 1946 game against Oklahoma State?

A. Thirteen.

Q. While playing against LSU in 1997, who set a new Razorback individual record for most yards gained in a single game?

A. Clint Stoerner (369 yards).

Q. Who broke Arkansas's 22-game winning streak with a 14–7 win in the 1966 Cotton Bowl game?

A. Louisiana State University.

Q. In 1929 what four-sport letterman from Pocahontas became Arkansas's first All-American in football?

A. Wear Schoonover.

Q. At 5'7" what was the weight of Arkansas's gridiron star George Cole?

A. 150 pounds.

Q. With how many punts returned did Razorback Ken Hatfield set an Arkansas individual record during the 1964 matchup with Rice?

A. Nine.

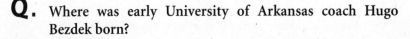

Q. Where was early University of Arkansas coach Hugo Bezdek born?

A. Prague, Bohemia.

Q. In the 1973 game against Baylor, what Razorback set a school individual record for most net rushing yards in a game?

A. Dickey Morton (271 yards in 28 rushes).

Q. By the 1920s what cheer became established for the University of Arkansas football games?

A. "Woo Pig Sooie."

Q. Over what color did the student body of 1894 select cardinal red for the school color?

A. Heliotrope (moderate purple).

Q. What Fayetteville businessman, in the first half of the twentieth century, billed himself as "the original No. 1 booster" of Razorback football?

A. Bill Sonneman.

Q. In the 1988 Arkansas vs. Mississippi game, how many sacks did Razorback Wayne Martin inflict against Ole Miss?

A. Five.

Q. What Razorback for the 1921–24 seasons went on to serve as a United States Senator representing the state of Arkansas from 1945–1974?

A. Bill Fulbright.

———— 🏈 ————

Q. With how many points did Arkansas quarterback George Cole set a one-season Razorback record in 1927 that stood until 1965?

A. Eighty-five.

———— 🏈 ————

Q. Coach John Barnhill lost what football great to the Mississippi Rebels, which caused him to exclude Mississippi from the Razorback's play schedule during the 1948–51 seasons?

A. John "Kayo" Dottley.

———— 🏈 ————

Q. Housed in the Broyles Athletic Center, what museum chronicles Razorback football?

A. Jerry Jones and Jim Lindsey Hall of Champions.

———— 🏈 ————

Q. In 1975 what facility was constructed at the north end of Razorback Stadium to house athletic administration and coaching staff?

A. The Broyles Athletic Center.

AUBURN

CHAPTER THREE

Auburn University was chartered in 1856 as the East Alabama Male College. Affiliated with the Methodist Church, the school opened as a private liberal arts institution in 1859. Due to the Civil War, the school closed in 1861. It reopened following the war but suffered such financial difficulties that the Methodist Church was forced to relinquish its property for the establishment of a new school. In 1872 the state legislature chartered the Agricultural and Mechanical College of Alabama, and the church holdings were transferred to state control. The new charter took advantage of the Morrill Act, making the school the first land-grant college in the South to be established separately from a state university.

The first women were admitted to the school in 1892, and a new name—Alabama Polytechnic Institute (API)—was applied to the college in 1899. During the early part of the twentieth century, API became the headquarters of the agricultural extension program in Alabama. Following World War II the school's enrollment experienced rapid growth fueled by returning veterans. The last half of the twentieth century brought about great change, including, in 1960, its present name, Auburn University.

Today twenty-some thousand undergraduate, graduate, and professional students are a part of Auburn's excellent academic programs. Baccalaureates are offered in over 130 areas through twelve colleges and schools with over seventy

AUBURN

academic departments. Auburn's Graduate School offers master's degrees in 130 areas with doctorates offered in almost 100 fields. The university features a faculty of more than 1,200 full-time members, plus over 8,000 staff, student workers, and administrators.

Jordan-Hare Stadium

Courtesy of Auburn University Athletic Media Relations

Q. Who is known as the "Father of Auburn Football"?

A. George Petrie.

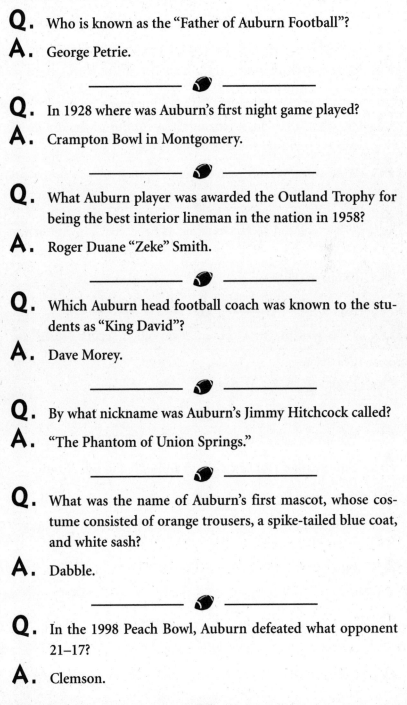

Q. In 1928 where was Auburn's first night game played?

A. Crampton Bowl in Montgomery.

Q. What Auburn player was awarded the Outland Trophy for being the best interior lineman in the nation in 1958?

A. Roger Duane "Zeke" Smith.

Q. Which Auburn head football coach was known to the students as "King David"?

A. Dave Morey.

Q. By what nickname was Auburn's Jimmy Hitchcock called?

A. "The Phantom of Union Springs."

Q. What was the name of Auburn's first mascot, whose costume consisted of orange trousers, a spike-tailed blue coat, and white sash?

A. Dabble.

Q. In the 1998 Peach Bowl, Auburn defeated what opponent 21–17?

A. Clemson.

AUBURN

Q. What was Bo Jackson's total rushing yardage while at Auburn?

A. 4,303 yards.

————————  ————————

Q. In what 1920 high-scoring 77–0 Auburn win did E. R. Moulton receive the nickname "Slick"?

A. Auburn vs. Washington & Lee.

————————  ————————

Q. Who replaced Mike Donahue as head coach at Auburn in 1923?

A. "Boozer" Pitts.

————————  ————————

Q. Who was the first center, then called "centre rush," for Auburn?

A. Professor Foster McKissick.

————————  ————————

Q. What two sets of twins played on the 1973 Auburn team?

A. Hamilin and Holley Caldwell and Bob and Bill Newton.

————————  ————————

Q. How many times was Auburn center Walter Gilbert selected as an All-American?

A. Three.

————————  ————————

Q. In 1942 Monk Gafford carried the ball 132 times for an average of how many yards per run?

A. 7.6.

Q. Where did Tommy Tuberville coach just prior to being named head football coach at Auburn on November 28, 1998?

A. University of Mississippi.

———— 🏈 ————

Q. Auburn and what SEC school did not play from 1908 to 1948 due to a contract dispute?

A. Alabama.

———— 🏈 ————

Q. Who became Auburn's head football coach in January of 1981?

A. Patrick Fain "Pat" Dye.

———— 🏈 ————

Q. What three Tigers were named All-American in 1994?

A. Frank Sanders, Chris Shelling, and Brian Robins.

———— 🏈 ————

Q. In the 1916 game against Georgia, from what piece of equipment did Moon Ducote kick a winning 48-yard field goal for Auburn?

A. His helmet.

———— 🏈 ————

Q. The first recorded use of the forward pass by Auburn was against what team in 1906?

A. Sewanee.

———— 🏈 ————

Q. What Auburn player was the No. 1 NFL draft pick in 1988?

A. Aundray Bruce (Atlanta Falcons).

AUBURN

Q. During the 1911 game against Georgia, how many Bulldog centers did "Sheep" Lamb knock unconscious?

A. Three.

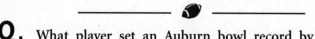

Q. What player set an Auburn bowl record by scoring 15 points at the 1954 Gator Bowl?

A. Joe Childress.

Q. Who was Auburn's first All-American?

A. Jimmy Hitchcock.

Q. The most coveted college football award is named for which early Auburn coach?

A. John W. Heisman (the Heisman Memorial Trophy).

Q. What Tiger was selected SEC Freshman of the Year for 1999?

A. Ronney Daniels.

Q. During his 1980–83 career at Auburn, kicker Al Del Greco nailed how many points between the goal posts?

A. 236.

Q. Who in 1944 became the second Auburn center to be named an All-American?

A. Tex Warrington.

Q. What Auburn quarterback led the nation in 1946 with 1,715 yards of total offense?

A. Travis Tidwell.

———————— 🏈 ————————

Q. Who was head football coach at Auburn from 1934 through 1942?

A. Jack Meagher.

———————— 🏈 ————————

Q. What great Auburn player was decorated for heroism during World War I for throwing himself on an enemy hand grenade to protect his men?

A. Kirk Newell.

———————— 🏈 ————————

Q. On New Year's Day 1996, who defeated Auburn 43–14 in the Outback Bowl?

A. Penn State.

———————— 🏈 ————————

Q. How was Auburn's mascot War Eagle II disposed of during the Depression because of the costs involved in taking care of him?

A. Donated to a traveling carnival.

———————— 🏈 ————————

Q. Where was the first Auburn-Alabama game played?

A. Lakeview Park, Birmingham.

———————— 🏈 ————————

Q. What was John Heisman's coaching record while at Auburn?

A. 12–4–2.

AUBURN

Q. Also referred to as the Rhumba Bowl or Cigar Bowl, where did Auburn play in its first bowl game on January 1, 1937?

A. The Bacardi Bowl, Havana, Cuba.

Q. Auburn's Travis Tidwell was first draft choice of what NFL team in 1950?

A. The New York Giants.

Q. Who was hired as head football coach at Auburn on February 26, 1951?

A. Ralph "Shug" Jordan.

Q. How many Auburn players were knocked unconscious during the 1908 game with LSU?

A. Three.

Q. What was the only team to score against Auburn in the 1910 season?

A. University of Texas.

Q. Who was the only married player on the 1986 Auburn team?

A. Brent Fullwood.

Q. What was the final score in Auburn's Gator Bowl victory over Colorado on December 30, 1972?

A. 24–3.

Q. What Auburn tailback was presented the Heisman Memorial Trophy in 1985?

A. Bo Jackson.

Q. On November 7, 1896, Auburn hosted its first on-campus game against what school?

A. Georgia Tech.

Q. Who was captain of Auburn's first and second football teams?

A. Frank Lupton.

Q. Who served as Auburn's fifth football coach, from 1895 through 1899?

A. John W. Heisman.

Q. What Auburn player originated the spiral pass from center in 1904?

A. Doc Bartlett.

Q. What Auburn defensive lineman was selected in the first round of the 1986 NFL draft by the Minnesota Vikings?

A. Gerald Robinson.

Q. What four Auburn linemen made All-Southern in 1914?

A. Dick Kearley, G. E. Taylor, J. H. Thigpen, and "Boozer" Pitts.

Q. In how many bowl games did Auburn appear while under the coaching of Ralph "Shug" Jordan?

A. Twelve.

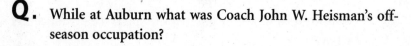

Q. In 1992–94 what Tiger kicker set a new Auburn record with a 44.41-yard career punting average?

A. Terry Daniel.

Q. What All-Southern lineman led Auburn with a 7–1 record to capture the 1919 Southern championship?

A. Pete Bonner.

Q. On what date was the first Auburn game played?

A. February 20, 1892.

Q. While at Auburn what was Coach John W. Heisman's off-season occupation?

A. Shakespearean actor.

Q. What was the final score in Auburn's 1969 victory over Alabama?

A. 49–26.

Q. What nickname was hung on Pat Sullivan by the press and his fans?

A. "Super Sully."

AUBURN

Q. In what two seasons was Auburn's Joe Childress selected All-SEC?

A. 1954 and 1955.

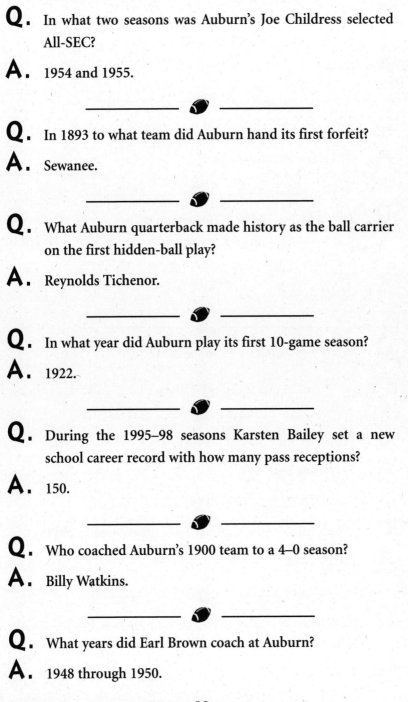

Q. In 1893 to what team did Auburn hand its first forfeit?

A. Sewanee.

Q. What Auburn quarterback made history as the ball carrier on the first hidden-ball play?

A. Reynolds Tichenor.

Q. In what year did Auburn play its first 10-game season?

A. 1922.

Q. During the 1995–98 seasons Karsten Bailey set a new school career record with how many pass receptions?

A. 150.

Q. Who coached Auburn's 1900 team to a 4–0 season?

A. Billy Watkins.

Q. What years did Earl Brown coach at Auburn?

A. 1948 through 1950.

AUBURN

Q. During the 1972–74 seasons how many punt return touchdowns did Mike Fuller score?

A. Three.

Q. Who scored the first touchdown in Auburn's football history?

A. R. T. "Dutch" Dorsey Jr.

Q. In 1988 what Auburn Tiger became the only SEC player to win both the Outland Trophy and the Lombardi Award in the same year?

A. Tracy Rocker.

Q. What was Auburn's 1950 season record?

A. 0–10.

Q. Who was Pat Sullivan's favorite receiver at Auburn?

A. Terry Beasley.

Q. What Auburn playing field was inaugurated in 1911?

A. Drake Field.

Q. The Heisman Memorial Trophy was presented to Pat Sullivan in what year?

A. 1971.

AUBURN

Q. From October 4, 1913, until November 13, 1915, how many games did Auburn play without a defeat?

A. Twenty-three.

———————— 🏈 ————————

Q. Auburn's War Eagle is what kind of bird?

A. A golden eagle.

———————— 🏈 ————————

Q. Coach Tommy Tuberville was a three-year letterman at what college?

A. Southern Arkansas University.

———————— 🏈 ————————

Q. In 1905 Auburn adopted what punishment for obscene or abusive language from players?

A. Mouths were to be washed out with soap.

———————— 🏈 ————————

Q. What was the distance of Connie Frederick's great run in the 1969 Auburn romp over Alabama?

A. Eighty-four yards.

———————— 🏈 ————————

Q. Where was the first Auburn football game played?

A. Piedmont Park, Atlanta.

———————— 🏈 ————————

Q. What two Auburn players were named to 1986 preseason All-American teams?

A. Tom Powell and Ben Tamburello.

Q. During what 1919 game at Drake Field did a bleacher collapse without any serious injuries to the 500 spectators who were sitting in them?

A. Auburn vs. The Fifth Division.

———— 🏈 ————

Q. What year became known as the X and Y year for Auburn due to the creation of two teams?

A. 1953.

———— 🏈 ————

Q. Auburn's great lineman Zeke Smith was a fullback at what high school?

A. Uniontown High, Uniontown, Alabama.

———— 🏈 ————

Q. Auburn's All-American lineman Ken Rice went on to play professional football with what team?

A. The Buffalo Bills.

———— 🏈 ————

Q. Where was the 1917 scoreless game between Auburn and Ohio State held?

A. Montgomery.

———— 🏈 ————

Q. Brent Fullwood rushed for how many yards during the 1986 season?

A. 1,391.

———— 🏈 ————

Q. What team did Auburn defeat 6–0 in the Orange Bowl on January 1, 1938?

A. Michigan State.

AUBURN

Q. When was the first Auburn-Alabama game played?

A. February 22, 1893.

———————— 🏈 ————————

Q. At what distance did John Riley in the 1969 Sun Bowl and Jaret Holmes in the 1998 Peach Bowl kick field goals for the Tigers?

A. Fifty-two yards.

———————— 🏈 ————————

Q. What former Auburn player served as governor of Alabama from 1979 to 1983?

A. Fob James.

———————— 🏈 ————————

Q. Jimmy Phillips was selected to play on how many All-American teams in 1957?

A. Eleven.

———————— 🏈 ————————

Q. What is Auburn's battle cry?

A. "War Eagle."

———————— 🏈 ————————

Q. Auburn's 1972 football team was given what nickname?

A. "The Amazin's."

———————— 🏈 ————————

Q. In what bowl did Auburn defeat the University of Southern California on January 1, 1987?

A. The Florida Citrus Bowl.

AUBURN

Q. The Auburn nickname "Tigers" is derived from what 1770 poem by Oliver Goldsmith?

A. "The Deserted Village."

———— 🏈 ————

Q. What Auburn coach originated the hidden ball play?

A. John W. Heisman.

———— 🏈 ————

Q. The Jacobs Award for Outstanding SEC Blocker was presented to what Auburn player in both 1963 and 1964?

A. Tucker Frederickson.

———— 🏈 ————

Q. How many consecutive home games did Auburn win between 1952 and 1960?

A. Thirty.

———— 🏈 ————

Q. What player led the Auburn team in touchdowns in 1910?

A. Bradley Streit.

———— 🏈 ————

Q. Over what team was Auburn victorious at the Gator Bowl on January 2, 1971?

A. Ole Miss.

———— 🏈 ————

Q. Against what university did Auburn first play?

A. University of Georgia.

Q. In 1960 how many field goals did Ed Dyas kick to set a NCAA single season record?

A. Thirteen.

Q. What Auburn All-American caught 34 passes in 1967, including a spectacular 70-yard touchdown against Kentucky?

A. Freddie Hyatt.

Q. Who did Auburn play during its first televised game (1954)?

A. Texas Tech.

Q. How many touchdowns did Tiger Ben Leard throw against Georgia in the 1999 game with the Bulldogs?

A. Four.

Q. How many consecutive games did Auburn play without suffering a defeat in the 1956, 1957, and 1958 seasons?

A. Twenty-four.

Q. What award is presented at the annual A-Day game to the Outstanding Senior Football Player of the Season?

A. The Shug Jordan Award.

Q. In his first year as head football coach at Auburn, who led the Tigers to an 11–0 season in 1993?

A. Terry Bowden.

Q. Just prior to the 1972 game between Auburn and Alabama, what term did Alabama coach "Bear" Bryant use to describe Auburn?

A. A "cow college."

————— 🏈 —————

Q. During the 1987 season what player accumulated the most passing yardage at Auburn since Pat Sullivan in 1971?

A. Jeff Burger (2,066).

————— 🏈 —————

Q. Auburn's 1892 64–0 loss to what school marks its worst defeat?

A. North Carolina.

————— 🏈 —————

Q. What punter set new Auburn records during the 1982 through 1985 seasons for career punts and most yards punted?

A. Lewis Colbert (244 punts; 10,179 yards).

————— 🏈 —————

Q. Who in 1902 was the first Auburn player to be selected All-Southern?

A. James Elmer.

————— 🏈 —————

Q. What kicker set Auburn's field goal record by kicking a 57-yard field goal against Tennessee in 1976?

A. Neil O'Donoghue.

————— 🏈 —————

Q. What was the price of admission to the first Auburn game?

A. Adults 50¢, children 25¢.

AUBURN

Q. Tiger Willie Gosha set a new Auburn single game individual record with how many pass receptions against Arkansas in the October 28, 1995 game?

A. Seventeen.

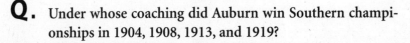

Q. Under whose coaching did Auburn win Southern championships in 1904, 1908, 1913, and 1919?

A. Mike Donahue.

Q. Who was selected Most Valuable Player in Auburn's win against Arizona in the 1986 Sun Bowl?

A. Buddy McClinton.

Q. Auburn's great receiver Terry Beasley was the first-round draft choice of what NFL team?

A. The San Francisco 49ers.

Q. What 1894 win represents Auburn's largest margin of victory?

A. 94–0 over Georgia Tech.

Q. What Auburn player became the first quarterback to lead the nation in rushing in 1963?

A. Jimmy Sidle.

Q. What was the final score in Auburn's first confrontation with Alabama?

A. Auburn 32–Alabama 22.

AUBURN

Q. What was Brent Fullwood's jersey number at Auburn?

A. Twenty-two.

———— 🏈 ————

Q. The 1970 56–0 win, Auburn's geatest margin of victory over an SEC opponent, was against which team?

A. Mississippi State.

———— 🏈 ————

Q. What are Auburn's team colors?

A. Burnt orange and navy blue.

———— 🏈 ————

Q. The 1987 season marked the end of the second oldest continuous game series in the Deep South between Auburn and what other team?

A. Georgia Tech.

———— 🏈 ————

Q. Where did Auburn's first team practice?

A. The drill field behind Samford Hall.

———— 🏈 ————

Q. How many games did Auburn play between October 4, 1982, and November 14, 1992, without being shut out?

A. 149 games.

———— 🏈 ————

Q. What name was given to Auburn's mascot War Eagle V?

A. Tiger.

———— 🏈 ————

Q. Who was the "one-game" coach who led Auburn to victory in its first encounter with Alabama?

A. F. M. Balliet.

FLORIDA

C H A P T E R   F O U R

The University of Florida stands as the state's largest, oldest, and most comprehensive university. The university traces its colorful history back to 1853 when the state-funded East Florida Seminary took over the facilities of Kingsbury Academy in Ocala. During the 1860s the seminary relocated to Gainesville. Later East Florida Seminary was merged with the state's land-grant Florida Agricultural College which was located in Lake City. By action of the state legislature in 1905, the college was officially declared a university, and Gainesville was chosen as the institution's new home. The first classes at the new location officially opened on September 26, 1906, with an all-male enrollment of 102 students. It would be another forty-one years before women would be allowed to enroll at the University of Florida.

In 1958 the university was integrated and today has one of the most culturally diverse student bodies in the nation. Over 100 countries and all fifty states are represented. Due to the phenomenal growth of enrollment at the University of Florida over the past century, the school is now ranked seventh in size nationally.

The campus covers some 2,000 acres, with 875 buildings. The campus facilities include such attractions as the Center for Performing Arts, Harn Museum of Art, University Art Galleries, and the Florida Museum of Natural History, which is one of the best in the nation. In addition the university is home to a microkelvin facility that has recorded the closest temperatures

FLORIDA

to absolute zero, a rare self-contained intensive-care hyperbaric chamber, and the world's largest citrus research center.

Around 125 undergraduate majors are offered at the University of Florida, with almost 200 graduate programs. Professional degree programs are offered in such fields as veterinary medicine, law, dentistry, medicine, and pharmacy.

Ben Hill Griffin Stadium at Florida Field

Courtesy of University of Florida Sports Information Department

Q. In what season did the University of Florida at Gainesville field its first football team?

A. 1906.

Q. In 1950 Coach Bob Woodruff spent $150 on what type of "special" equipment for the Florida team when playing Kentucky in the snow at Lexington?

A. Long "long-handle" underwear.

Q. At 6'2" and 220 pounds, who was the largest member of the 1938 Florida team?

A. Clark Goff.

Q. Under what coach did Florida clinch its first-ever first place SEC finish?

A. Galen Hall.

Q. What Florida assistant football coach went on to become a successful head coach at Arkansas?

A. Frank Broyles.

Q. At 194 points, what player holds the Florida record for the highest scoring by a nonkicker?

A. Neal Anderson.

Q. What Florida guard was selected All-Southern in 1930?

A. James Steele.

FLORIDA

Q. What was the combined number of points scored by Florida during the 1916, 1918, 1946, and 1979 seasons?

A. Zero.

————— 🏈 —————

Q. Florida's great Walter Mayberry suffered what injury while playing high school football at Daytona Beach?

A. A broken neck.

————— 🏈 —————

Q. What record did Coach Ray Graves compile during his ten years with Florida?

A. 70–31–4.

————— 🏈 —————

Q. What ambidextrous quarterback played at Florida from 1927 through 1929?

A. Clyde "Cannonball" Crabtree.

————— 🏈 —————

Q. What year was Steve Spurrier's first season as head football coach at Florida?

A. 1990.

————— 🏈 —————

Q. What Gator posted an impressive total of 5,393 yards gained during his 1990–93 career at Florida?

A. Errict Rhett.

————— 🏈 —————

Q. Roy Corbett was not only captain of the 1907 team but also served as athletics editor of what campus publication?

A. The *Florida Pennant*.

Q. What was Douglas Adair "Doug" Dickey's first season as head football coach at Florida?

A. 1970.

Q. What Gator carried the ball 189 times during the 1963 season?

A. Larry DuPree.

Q. Who coached Florida football from 1909 through 1913?

A. G. E. Pyle.

Q. How many 300-plus-yard passing games did Kerwin Bell have during the 1985 season?

A. Three.

Q. What was coach Bob Woodruff's battle cry?

A. "Oski Wow-Wow."

Q. A 13-game losing streak for Florida ended on October 8, 1947, with a 7–6 victory over what school?

A. North Carolina State.

Q. What newcomer to the 1907 football team later became a noted state legislator?

A. W. A. "Bill" Shands.

Q. By what nickname is the Florida football team called?

A. Gators, short for Alligators.

———— 🏈 ————

Q. What school defeated Florida 37–34 in the 2000 Florida Citrus Bowl?

A. Michigan State.

———— 🏈 ————

Q. Forest "Fergie" Ferguson was not only one of Florida's great football players, but he set an AAU record in what track-and-field event?

A. Javelin throw.

———— 🏈 ————

Q. Who followed Doug Dickey as head football coach at Florida?

A. Charley Pell.

———— 🏈 ————

Q. Of the 1,202 passes thrown by Shane Matthews during his 1989–92 career at Florida, how many were completed?

A. 722.

———— 🏈 ————

Q. What was "Chuck" Hunsinger's jersey number?

A. Forty-six.

———— 🏈 ————

Q. How many touchdown catches did Carlos Alvarez make during Florida's 1969 game with Vanderbilt?

A. Three.

FLORIDA

Q. What versatile player captained the 1935 Florida football team?

A. Billy Chase.

―――――― 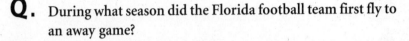 ――――――

Q. During what season did the Florida football team first fly to an away game?

A. 1947 season, to New Orleans.

―――――― 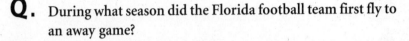 ――――――

Q. Where did Ray Graves sign his contract with Florida to become head football coach?

A. The Holiday Inn at Gainesville.

―――――― 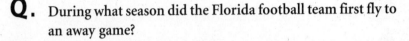 ――――――

Q. Who captained the 1927 team to a 33–6 win over Auburn?

A. William "Wee Willie" Middlekauf.

―――――― 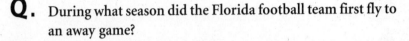 ――――――

Q. What Florida halfback was immortalized in song by *Birmingham News* sports editors Zipp Newman and Earl Crumly?

A. Charles Ray "Chuck" Hunsinger: "The Hunsinger Song."

―――――― 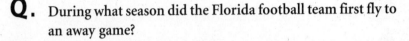 ――――――

Q. Who set a Florida record of 117 consecutive passes without an interception in 1981?

A. Wayne Peace.

―――――― 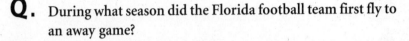 ――――――

Q. In addition to $120.37 for expenses, what amount of salary did Coach G. E. Pyle receive during his last year at Florida?

A. $410.87.

FLORIDA

Q. During the 1957 season what game did Florida fans consider its biggest upset win?

A. A 22–14 victory over LSU.

———— 🏈 ————

Q. What was the full name of Florida's Carlos Alvarez?

A. Carlos Alvarez Vasquez Rodriquez Ubieta.

———— 🏈 ————

Q. How many consecutive games did Thomas Johnson "John" Reaves play during his three Florida seasons?

A. Thirty-three.

———— 🏈 ————

Q. William G. Kline, who coached Florida football from 1920 through 1922, held a degree in what area?

A. Law.

———— 🏈 ————

Q. What 1977 Florida quarterback became a Rhodes Scholar?

A. Bill Kynes.

———— 🏈 ————

Q. What two Gator defensive backs earned first-team All-American honors in 1987?

A. Louis Oliver and Jarvis Williams.

———— 🏈 ————

Q. For what annual salary was Coach Bob Woodruff hired in 1950?

A. $17,000.

Q. Who did Florida defeat in the 1997 Sugar Bowl?

A. Florida State (52–20).

———— 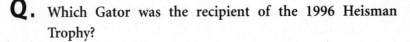 ————

Q. Wilber Marshall was first-round draft choice of what NFL team in 1984?

A. Chicago Bears.

———— ————

Q. What was the only game for Florida in the 1918 season?

A. Florida vs. Camp Johnson.

———— ————

Q. With what professional football team did Florida's great defensive end Jack Youngblood receive All-Pro star honors?

A. The Los Angeles Rams.

———— ————

Q. What was the season record of the spectacular 1928 team?

A. 8–1–0.

———— ————

Q. What talented guard became the first Florida football player to receive a scholarship from the Hebrew Club in Jacksonville?

A. Goldy Goldstein.

———— ————

Q. Which Gator was the recipient of the 1996 Heisman Trophy?

A. Danny Wuerffel.

Q. What 1980 All-American linebacker made 375 tackles during his Florida career?

A. David Little.

———— 🏈 ————

Q. At the end of the 1912 season, what two teams did Florida confront during its first and last venture to Cuba?

A. The Vedado Club and a partial game with the Cuban Athletic Club.

———— 🏈 ————

Q. Steve Spurrier became the first player in the history of the Sugar Bowl to receive what honor while on the losing team?

A. Most Valuable Player.

———— 🏈 ————

Q. What Florida football coach of the 1923 and 1924 seasons went on to become a four-star general?

A. James A. Van Fleet.

———— 🏈 ————

Q. Who beat Florida 62–24 in the 1996 Fiesta Bowl?

A. Nebraska.

———— 🏈 ————

Q. What was the total of gate receipts for Florida during the seven-game 1913 season?

A. $3,082.71.

———— 🏈 ————

Q. In 1939 who became the first player to represent Florida at the Blue-Gray Classic in Montgomery?

A. Clarke Goff.

FLORIDA

Q. What was coach G. E. Pyle's record at Florida?

A. 26–10–3.

Q. What 1965 Florida All-American offensive guard later played for the Kansas City Chiefs?

A. Larry Gagner.

Q. Setting a record, how many yards did Emmitt Smith rush in the 1989 matchup with New Mexico?

A. 316.

Q. Who is regarded as the best defensive end in the history of Florida football?

A. Jack Youngblood.

Q. What Florida offensive line coach later became head coach at Wichita State and Texas A&M?

A. Hank Foldberg.

Q. In 1937 who became Florida's first All-SEC player?

A. Walter Mayberry.

Q. During what 1952 game did Florida intercept a record six passes?

A. Florida vs. Clemson.

Q. Who selected the alligator emblem to represent the Florida football team in the fall of 1907?

A. Austin Miller.

Q. In the 1999 Orange Bowl, Florida defeated what opponent 31–10?

A. Syracuse.

Q. What assistant football coach to Bob Woodruff later became the head coach of the Buffalo Bills?

A. John Rauch.

Q. What Florida offensive guard was selected first-team All-American by both the Walter Camp Football Foundation and the *Sporting News* in 1985?

A. Jeff Zimmerman.

Q. What seasons did the great R. D. "Ark" Newton play football at Florida?

A. 1921 through 1924.

Q. Who was the captain of the 1914 team who was sidelined due to a heart condition after the season opener?

A. John Sutton.

Q. Who in 1975 became the first black Florida player to receive first-team All-American honors?

A. Sammy Green.

Q. Tom Leib, who coached Florida football from 1940 through 1945, was an Olympic champion in what event?

A. Discus.

———— 🏈 ————

Q. Outside linebacker Alonzo Johnson received what recognition from the *Sporting News* for his 1984 and 1985 seasons at Florida?

A. First-team All-American, both years.

———— 🏈 ————

Q. What team was defeated by Florida at the 1967 Orange Bowl game?

A. Georgia Tech (27–12).

———— 🏈 ————

Q. Who was hired on January 6, 1950, as head football coach and athletic director at Florida?

A. Bob Woodruff.

———— 🏈 ————

Q. What 1956 Florida All-American and All-SEC player later became All-Canadian Football League lineman with Hamilton?

A. John Barrow.

———— 🏈 ————

Q. Tonto Coleman, who coached Florida freshmen during the '50s, later held what position with the Southeastern Conference?

A. Commissioner.

———— 🏈 ————

Q. What governor pledged during his campaign to try to get a winning football team at Florida?

A. Fuller Warren.

Q. Against what team on October 6, 1913, did Florida score a 144–0 win?

A. Florida Southern.

———— 🏈 ————

Q. In 1993 what Gator was the recipient of the Lou Groza National Place Kicker of the Year award?

A. Judd Davis.

———— 🏈 ————

Q. What Florida player was selected ABC-TV (Chevrolet) "Defensive Player of the Year" in 1983?

A. Wilber Marshall.

———— 🏈 ————

Q. Who in 1928 became Florida's first All-American?

A. Dale Vansickle.

———— 🏈 ————

Q. Who coached the first University of Florida football team at Gainesville?

A. J. A. "Pee Wee" Forsythe Jr.

———— 🏈 ————

Q. As college football's Most Outstanding Player for 1966, what prestigious award was bestowed upon Steve Spurrier by a landslide vote?

A. The Heisman Memorial Trophy.

———— 🏈 ————

Q. Who was the head football coach at Florida during the 1946–49 seasons?

A. Ray "Bear" Wolf.

Q. How many times did Larry DuPree earn first-team All-SEC honors?

A. Three.

———————— 🏈 ————————

Q. The Gators handed what team a 27–10 defeat in the 1992 Gator Bowl?

A. North Carolina State.

———————— 🏈 ————————

Q. Who did Coach Bob Woodruff refer to as being "pound-for-pound" the best player he ever coached?

A. Jimmy Dunn.

———————— 🏈 ————————

Q. The Florida Sportswriters Association presented what award to Kerwin Bell in 1985?

A. "Amateur Athlete of the Year."

———————— 🏈 ————————

Q. Against what team did Florida win its first victory over a major out-of-state college on October 19, 1922?

A. South Carolina.

———————— 🏈 ————————

Q. What was Walter Mayberry's nickname?

A. "Tiger."

———————— 🏈 ————————

Q. During the twentieth century how many Gators were selected in first-round drafts of the NFL?

A. Thirty-one.

Q. Who in 1970 set a Florida season record for most kickoff returns with 23?

A. Willie Jackson.

Q. How many fumbles did Florida recover in 1972 and again in 1975?

A. Twenty-five.

Q. What 1984 All-American and All-SEC Florida tackle was a first-round draft choice of the Detroit Lions?

A. Lomas Brown.

Q. Florida's 1969 star defensive back Steve Tannen played for what NFL team?

A. New York Jets.

Q. What type of decals did Florida players stick on their helmets when they confronted Penn State in 1962?

A. Confederate flags.

Q. At the hands of what school did Florida suffer its worst lopsided defeat in 1942?

A. Georgia (75–0).

Q. Where had Charles J. McCoy coached just prior to becoming a football coach at Florida in October of 1914?

A. Sewanee Military Academy.

Q. With how many points did Florida lead the nation during the 1928 season?

A. 336.

Q. What Gator safety received the prestigious Thorpe Award in 1996?

A. Lawrence Wright.

Q. Where did Florida play in its first bowl game?

A. The Gator Bowl (1953, Florida 14–Tulsa 13).

Q. Who was the star quarterback of the 18–17 Florida upset of Georgia Tech in 1960?

A. Larry Libertore.

Q. What was the final score in Florida's 1983 Gator Bowl win over Iowa?

A. 14–6.

Q. Who was captain of Florida's first team at Gainesville?

A. Thomas Guy Hancock.

Q. During the 1977 game between Florida and Rice, what Gator tied the NCAA record for longest touchdown pass?

A. Cris Collinsworth (99 yards).

Q. Due to World War II, in what year did Florida not field a team?

A. 1943.

Q. Who set a Florida season record in 1969 with 18 touchdowns?

A. Tommy Durrance.

———— 🏈 ————

Q. Whom did coach Bob Woodruff call his "smartest" quarterback?

A. Doug Dickey.

———— 🏈 ————

Q. What two Florida players received first-team All-American awards in 1974?

A. Burton Lawless and Ralph Ortega.

———— 🏈 ————

Q. How many first downs did Florida make during the 1967 Tulane game?

A. Thirty-two.

———— 🏈 ————

Q. What head football coach at Florida later became the chief justice of the state supreme court?

A. H. L. "Tom" Sebring.

———— 🏈 ————

Q. What Florida kicker received an Academic All-American award in 1976?

A. David Posey.

Q. Which Gator defensive tackle was recognized as National Defensive Player of the Year in 1994?

A. Ellis Johnson.

Q. On what date did Florida play its first bowl game?

A. January 1, 1953 (against Tulsa).

Q. What Gator ran for 1,725 yards during the 1962–64 seasons?

A. Larry DuPree.

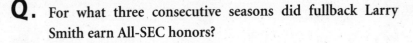

Q. During the 1995–97 seasons Gator Jacquez Green set a Florida career record with how many punt return touchdowns?

A. Four.

Q. For what three consecutive seasons did fullback Larry Smith earn All-SEC honors?

A. 1966–68.

Q. How long was freshman sensation Emmitt Smith's first collegiate touchdown run in 1987?

A. Sixty-six yards (against Tulsa).

Q. What All-SEC receiver caught 58 passes in 1965?

A. Charles Casey.

Q. Against what school did Florida play its first football game?

A. Rollins.

———————— 🏈 ————————

Q. Dale VanSickle later had a successful career in what area of the motion picture industry?

A. A stunt man.

———————— 🏈 ————————

Q. What was the length of Hal Griffin's 1946 punt return touchdown against Miami?

A. Ninety-seven yards.

———————— 🏈 ————————

Q. When did Florida first play Florida State?

A. November 22, 1958.

———————— 🏈 ————————

Q. Who holds the Florida career record for most field goal attempts?

A. Brian Clark (63 attempts).

———————— 🏈 ————————

Q. At what 1910 away game was the Florida football team escorted back to their train under police protection following a 33–0 win?

A. Florida vs. Columbia College at Lake City.

GEORGIA

CHAPTER FIVE

The American system of public higher education owes its origin to the Georgia legislature. On January 27, 1785, the Georgia General Assembly voted to charter the nation's first state-supported university, and the University of Georgia was born on paper. In February 1786 the school's board of trustees met in Augusta and selected Abraham Baldwin as the university's first president, but it would be several more years before the university actually opened its doors for business. In 1787 the author of the university's charter Abraham Baldwin and university board of trustees member William Few both represented Georgia and signed the Constitution of the United States of America at the Constitutional Convention in Philadelphia, Pennsylvania.

In 1801 the actual establishment of the university came about when John Milledge, later a governor of Georgia, purchased and donated a 633-acre tract of land on the banks of the Oconee River to the board of trustees. A new university president, Josiah Meigs, was selected and construction began on the first building. This facility was originally named Franklin College in honor of Benjamin Franklin but later became known as Old College. In 1804 the first class graduated from the University of Georgia.

In 1843 courses in law were introduced at the University of Georgia. Until that time the curriculum consisted of traditional classical studies. As was the case with many institutes of higher learning in the South, the Civil War brought about unique and challenging circumstances for the university. Stability slowly returned following the war, and in 1872 the university received funds from the federal government to open studies in agriculture and mechanical arts. The remainder of the nineteenth century saw new opportunities added to the curriculum, but the greatest and most rapid growth in programs and enrollment came during the twentieth century.

From 1850 through the end of the twentieth century, twenty-four of Georgia's governors were graduates of the University of Georgia. Today it continues developing leaders in the fields of government, science, the arts, education, and sports.

Sanford Stadium

Courtesy of University of Georgia Sports Communications

GEORGIA

Q. Who was selected Georgia's first All-American football player?

A. Bob McWhorter.

───────── 🏈 ─────────

Q. Best All Around Offensive Player was awarded to what Bulldog during the 1986 Spring Awards?

A. Wilbur Strozier.

───────── 🏈 ─────────

Q. The first game played at Sanford Stadium was a 15–0 victory for the Bulldogs over what school?

A. Yale.

───────── 🏈 ─────────

Q. Into what bowl did Vince Dooley lead the "Dogs" his first season at Georgia?

A. Sun Bowl (1964).

───────── 🏈 ─────────

Q. The jerseys of what legendary Georgia Bulldogs have been officially retired?

A. Frank Sinkwich (21), Charley Trippi (62), Theron Sapp (40), and Herschel Walker (34).

───────── 🏈 ─────────

Q. Who served the Bulldogs as head coach from 1928 to 1937?

A. Harry Mehre.

───────── 🏈 ─────────

Q. What Georgia player in 1987 broke Herschel Walker's school record for all-purpose yards in a single game?

A. Rodney Hampton (283 yards against Ole Miss).

Q. What academic honor was bestowed on Bulldog Tommy Lawhorne in 1968?

A. Valedictorian of the Senior Class.

———————— 🏈 ————————

Q. What Bulldog scored five touchdowns in Georgia's 1995 bout with South Carolina?

A. Robert Edwards.

———————— 🏈 ————————

Q. Who served as team captain for Coach Wally Butts in his final season at Georgia?

A. Fran Tarkenton.

———————— 🏈 ————————

Q. What was the nickname of kicking specialist George Jernigan?

A. "Goat."

———————— 🏈 ————————

Q. What mascot serves the University of Georgia?

A. An English bulldog.

———————— 🏈 ————————

Q. Which Bulldog head football coach was born in Laurens, South Carolina, on January 29, 1945?

A. Jim "James" Donnan.

———————— 🏈 ————————

Q. The inaugural game at Sanford Stadium was played in what year?

A. 1929.

Q. What fullback was known in 1957 as "The Man Who Broke the Drought"?

A. Theron Sapp.

Q. What are the Bulldog colors?

A. Red and black.

Q. Coming back from a 21-point second-quarter deficit, Georgia went on to a 35–33 victory over what 1998 Peach Bowl opponent?

A. Virginia.

Q. Sanford Stadium has what type of playing surface?

A. Natural grass.

Q. Following his collegiate years at Georgia, Fran Tarkenton quarterbacked what NFL teams?

A. Minnesota Vikings and New York Giants.

Q. Who was the first full-time salaried coach at Georgia?

A. Coach "Pop" Warner.

Q. What individual was named Outstanding Walk-On for spring 1986?

A. Richard Fromm.

GEORGIA

Q. Bob McWhorter scored how many touchdowns during his 33-game career at Georgia?

A. Sixty-one.

———— 🏈 ————

Q. What is the number of Herschel Walker's retired jersey?

A. Thirty-four.

———— 🏈 ————

Q. In what 2000 bowl game did the Bulldogs make an incredible twenty-five point comeback to win 28–25 over Purdue?

A. Outback Bowl.

———— 🏈 ————

Q. What Bulldog became captain and star quarterback of the 1911 Georgia team?

A. George "Kid" Woodruff.

———— 🏈 ————

Q. What Georgia letterman later became the leading scorer with the Philadelphia Eagles?

A. Bobby Walston.

———— 🏈 ————

Q. Who succeeded Wally Butts as head coach in 1961?

A. Johnny Griffith.

———— 🏈 ————

Q. What is the name of the Georgia marching band that adds color and music to Bulldog football games?

A. Georgia Redcoat Marching Band.

Q. In how many bowl contests did Charley Trippi lead the Bulldogs to victory?

A. Three: Rose, Oil, and Sugar Bowls.

―――――――― 🏈 ――――――――

Q. In what year was Sanford Stadium double-decked?

A. 1967.

―――――――― 🏈 ――――――――

Q. In what year was Georgia tagged as the "Dream and Wonder Team"?

A. 1927.

―――――――― 🏈 ――――――――

Q. What seasons did Ray Goff serve as head football coach at Georgia?

A. 1989–95.

―――――――― 🏈 ――――――――

Q. What Georgia placekicker booted a 39-yard field goal with no time left on the clock to defeat Arkansas 20–17 in the 1987 Liberty Bowl?

A. Freshman John Kasay.

―――――――― 🏈 ――――――――

Q. Who is known as the "Father of Georgia Football"?

A. Dr. Charles Herty.

―――――――― 🏈 ――――――――

Q. By the end of the 1984 campaign, a new SEC record had been set by what Bulldog for most points scored in a career?

A. Kevin Butler.

Q. How was football saved in the south following the death of Georgia fullback Richard Von Gammon in 1897?

A. Von Gammon's mother wrote a letter to her state representative in defense of the game.

———— 🏈 ————

Q. What former 1968 Georgia Bulldogs once again became teammates playing for the Miami Dolphins, both receiving All-Pro honors?

A. Bill Stanfill and Jake Scott.

———— 🏈 ————

Q. The 1927 "Dream and Wonder Team" won its first nine games but lost in the season finale to what school?

A. Georgia Tech.

———— 🏈 ————

Q. In the 22nd Peach Bowl on December 30, 1989, Georgia suffered a one point defeat by what school?

A. Syracuse.

———— 🏈 ————

Q. What Bulldog coach was inducted into the Georgia Sports Hall of Fame (1978) and the Alabama Sports Hall of Fame (1984)?

A. Vince Dooley.

———— 🏈 ————

Q. What Bulldog quarterback played two years in the Chicago Cubs baseball organization prior to enrolling at the University of Georgia?

A. Quincy Carter.

———— 🏈 ————

Q. Herschel Walker set how many school records during his football career at Georgia?

A. Forty-one.

GEORGIA

Q. Attired in a black coat with red U.G. letters, what animal served as mascot at Georgia's first football game in 1892?

A. A goat.

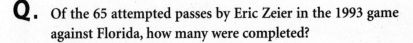

Q. Of the 65 attempted passes by Eric Zeier in the 1993 game against Florida, how many were completed?

A. Thirty-six.

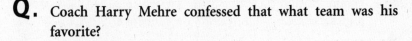

Q. What school played Georgia to a 0–0 tie in the 1938 Homecoming game?

A. Georgia Tech.

———— 🏈 ————

Q. Coach Harry Mehre confessed that what team was his favorite?

A. The 1929 "Flaming Sophomores."

———— 🏈 ————

Q. What Bulldog played in the 1942 Orange Bowl wearing a mask that protected a broken jaw?

A. Frankie Sinkwich.

———— 🏈 ————

Q. Who set a Georgia season record for most touchdowns?

A. Garrison Hearst (21 touchdowns).

———— 🏈 ————

Q. What former Georgia governor served as substitute quarterback in the 1945 Oil Bowl?

A. Carl E. Sanders.

Q. During his 1991–94 seasons as a Bulldog, Eric Zeier set a Georgia career record with how many pass completions?

A. 838.

Q. Who was the first coach in the south to utilize the T-formation as the basic formation?

A. Wally Butts.

Q. Rushing 27 times for a net gain of 115 yards, what Bulldog received the Helms Award in the 1943 Rose Bowl?

A. Sophomore Charley Trippi.

Q. What motion picture actress invited the 1943 Rose Bowl-bound team to a Hollywood party prior to the game?

A. Rita Hayworth.

Q. Former Bulldog Len Hauss was named All-Pro in 1974 while playing center for what NFL team?

A. Washington Redskins.

Q. Vernon Smith of the legendary "Flaming Sophomores" was known by what nickname?

A. "Catfish."

Q. In 1997 during how many touchdown passes did Mike Bobo throw during Georgia's matchup with Georgia Tech?

A. Four.

GEORGIA

Q. Just prior to coming to Georgia in 1996, where had Jim Donnan served as head football coach?

A. Marshall University.

———— 🏈 ————

Q. Coach Wally Butts was named SEC Coach of the Year how many times?

A. Three: 1942, 1946, and 1959.

———— 🏈 ————

Q. What Georgia All-American was nicknamed "the Brat"?

A. Zeke Bratkowski.

———— 🏈 ————

Q. What was the name of Georgia's solid white bull terrier mascot of 1894?

A. Trilby.

———— 🏈 ————

Q. What 1987 freshman running back started more games than any freshman since Herschel Walker in 1980?

A. Fullback Alphonso Ellis (10 games).

———— 🏈 ————

Q. In the 24–17 victory over LSU in 1978, what freshman set a new school record with a 99-yard kickoff return?

A. Lindsay Scott.

———— 🏈 ————

Q. What Bulldog was the son of a former Georgia All-American and Miami Dolphin All-Pro?

A. Stan Stanfill, son of Bill Stanfill.

GEORGIA

Q. In 1954 who became the fist Georgia player to be named to the National Football Hall of Fame?

A. Bob McWhorter.

Q. What 1986 Georgia football signee was named third best player in the state by the Atlanta *Journal-Consititution*?

A. Mark Fletcher.

Q. Who set a Georgia record with 15 receptions in the 1993 game with Florida?

A. Shannon Mitchell.

Q. In 1993 what Bulldog set a Georgia season record with 76 receptions?

A. Brice Hunter.

Q. Who served as captain of the first Vince Dooley squad?

A. Barry Wilson.

Q. In 1942 what Bulldog became the south's first Heisman Trophy recipient?

A. Frank Sinkwich.

Q. The Bulldogs put the bite on the Razorbacks in what 1991 bowl game?

A. Independence Bowl (24–15).

Q. The Wallace Butts Memorial Award, awarded to the player who "best pays the price" for success, was given to what linebacker in 1984?

A. Knox Culpepper.

———— 🏈 ————

Q. When did the Georgia Bulldogs first gain national recognition?

A. 1929, in the 15–0 game over Yale.

———— 🏈 ————

Q. With what pro football team did Charley Trippi sign following the 1947 Sugar Bowl?

A. Chicago Cardinals.

———— 🏈 ————

Q. Who received the 1986 Spring Award for Best Tackler?

A. Steve Boswell.

———— 🏈 ————

Q. During the 1986 season what individual made the longest run from scrimmage in a single game?

A. Keith Henderson (50 yards).

———— 🏈 ————

Q. What years did Butch, a brindled English bulldog, serve as mascot at Georgia?

A. 1947–50.

———— 🏈 ————

Q. Wealthy Columbus businessman George Woodruff coached the Bulldogs from 1923 through 1927 for what yearly salary?

A. One dollar.

GEORGIA

Q. What captain of the 1937 Bulldogs was selected by Wally Butts to coach the backfield in 1939?

A. Bill Hartman.

Q. What roverback was honored as Academic All-SEC from Georgia in 1984, 1985, and 1986?

A. John Little.

Q. Vince Dooley was bestowed what great coaching honor in 1980?

A. NCAA National Coach of the Year.

Q. Quarterback Bill Hartman was drafted by what NFL team in 1938?

A. Washington Redskins.

Q. What receiver did Wally Butts say was the most outstanding he had ever coached?

A. Lamar Davis.

Q. Having never played football until 1985, what Bulldog was offered a scholarship by Coach Vince Dooley that same year?

A. Richard Tardits.

Q. How many points did Herschel Walker score during his career (1980–82), setting a school and SEC record?

A. 314.

GEORGIA

Q. At the 1986 homecoming over what team was Georgia victorious?

A. Richmond.

———— 🏈 ————

Q. For what early Georgia faculty member, founder of the Henry W. Grady School of Journalism, and later dean, president, and chancellor of UGA was Sanford Stadium named?

A. Dr. Steadman V. Sanford.

———— 🏈 ————

Q. Former Bulldogs Peter Anderson and Ray Donaldson became teammates again on what NFL team?

A. Indianapolis Colts.

———— 🏈 ————

Q. In the 1907 campaign against Georgia Tech, what Georgia coach had to make a timely exit because of illegal recruiting?

A. W. S. Whitney.

———— 🏈 ————

Q. What man last served as a four-letter coach of the Bulldogs, coaching basketball, golf, track, and football?

A. H. J. Stegeman (1920–22).

———— 🏈 ————

Q. What Bulldog became the school's second All-American in 1923?

A. Joe Bennett.

———— 🏈 ————

Q. What year did Georgia Tech defeat Georgia, causing Bulldog fans to claim the Tech coach watered down the field?

A. 1927.

Q. Terry Hoage was drafted by what NFL team in 1984?

A. New Orleans Saints.

Q. After World War II what former Georgia football head coach returned to the school as instructor and advisor to veterans?

A. W. A. "Alex" Cunningham.

Q. Brice Hunter in 1993, Hason Graham in 1994, and Terrence Edwards in 1999 all had how many touchdown receptions?

A. Nine.

Q. Known as the "Voice of the Dogs," who started calling the Bulldog play-by-play in 1966?

A. Larry Munson.

Q. Kevin Butler scored how many points during his 1981–84 career at Georgia?

A. 353.

Q. What former Bulldog played offensive tackle for the New York Giants, winning an NFL World Championship in 1956?

A. Dick Yelvington.

Q. The Bulldogs chewed up what team 33–6 in the 1998 Outback Bowl?

A. Wisconsin.

Q. In what year did Georgia score a perfect season and a Sugar Bowl win?

A. 1946.

Q. At the end of the 1980 and 1982 seasons, Vince Dooley was selected to receive what national award?

A. NCAA Coach of the Year.

Q. Alfred Anderson of the 1934–36 Bulldogs completed his Georgia football career to become a major league infielder for what club?

A. Pittsburgh.

Q. Bulldog Hap Hines kicked how many field goals in the 1999 game with Ole Miss?

A. Four.

Q. The Bulldogs played their first bowl contest in what bowl?

A. 1942 Orange Bowl.

Q. In 1985 what former Bulldog placekicker was added to the list of NFL World Champions?

A. Kevin Butler.

Q. In 1985 Georgia received what annual award given to the most successful men's athletic program in the SEC?

A. The Bernie Moore Trophy.

Q. In his first collegiate game, what 1930s Bulldog scored the first three times he had possession of the ball?

A. Buster Mott.

————  ————

Q. The Georgia Bulldogs were SEC Champions for what three consecutive years?

A. 1980, 1981, and 1982.

————  ————

Q. Who was chosen by Coach Harry Mehre as the greatest lineman ever to play for him at Georgia or Ole Miss?

A. Quinton Lumpkin.

————  ————

Q. Wayne Radloff of the Atlanta Falcons received All-SEC honors in what year?

A. 1982.

————  ————

Q. In what 1995 bowl game did a touchdown by Virginia with 57 seconds remaining doom Georgia to a 27–34 loss?

A. Peach Bowl.

————  ————

Q. In 1981 how many touchdowns did Herschel Walker make, setting an SEC season record?

A. Twenty.

————  ————

Q. First surfacing in the mid to late 1970s, what Georgia slogan went nationwide via a major wire service following the Bulldogs' 1980 victory over Notre Dame?

A. "How 'Bout Them Dogs!"

Q. During the 1993 season Bulldog Mitch Davis totaled up how many sacks against Georgia opponents?

A. Thirteen.

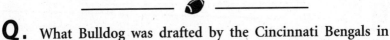

Q. What Bulldog was drafted by the Cincinnati Bengals in 1980?

A. Rex Robinson.

Q. In what year was Uga I made the official mascot of the university?

A. 1956.

Q. What Bulldogs were selected for All-SEC honors in 1985?

A. Peter Anderson, Tony Flack, Greg Waters, and John Little.

Q. What Bulldog was named Most Valuable Player of the 1964 Sun Bowl?

A. Preston Ridlehuber.

Q. During his 1974–77 career, what individual set the Georgia record for most career total tackles?

A. Ben Zambiasi.

Q. The Georgia Bulldog Hall of Fame is housed in what facility?

A. McWhorter Hall.

Q. Coach Wally Butts chose what game as the best he ever coached?

A. The 1924 34–0 victory over Georgia Tech.

Q. Who was the 1986 Bulldog defensive anchor?

A. John Little, All-American roverback.

Q. What Georgia fullback received a Chevrolet Scholarship Award against Alabama in 1984?

A. Andre Smith.

Q. How many points did Herschel Walker score when he broke the school record for most points scored in a game in 1981?

A. Twenty-four.

Q. In 1951, 1952, and 1953 Vince Dooley played for what SEC school?

A. Auburn.

Q. What coach first brought the Bulldogs national attention?

A. Harry Mehre.

KENTUCKY

CHAPTER SIX

The University of Kentucky has a convoluted and fascinating heritage. In 1865 the state of Kentucky established the Agricultural and Mechanical College of the Kentucky University as a land-grant institution. The Kentucky University was founded in 1858 at Harrodsburg. In 1865 Kentucky University merged with Transylvania University of Lexington. In 1878 the state separated the Agriculture and Mechanical College from the Kentucky University and the following year officially established the Agricultural and Mechanical College of Kentucky. In addition to state monies, the city of Lexington provided funds and donated the city park for use as a campus for the newly designated school.

With the opening of a Normal Department in 1880, the first women students were enrolled. Degrees were not initially available to women, but in 1888 A&M saw its first women graduates.

In 1908 the college was renamed State University, Lexington, Kentucky. To avoid confusion, Kentucky University reverted to using the name Transylvania University. Eight years later, in 1916, State University became the University of Kentucky. The main campus is situated on 673 acres just south of downtown Lexington. The University of Kentucky's academic roster is comprised of sixteen colleges and a graduate school offering almost 100 master's degree programs and some sixty doctoral programs. In addition the university maintains over twenty research centers and the university hospital.

Today's 30,000 plus enrollment includes students from every state and more than 100 countries. There are 1,800 plus full-time faculty members, 98 percent of which hold the highest possible degrees in their given fields. Throughout its colorful history the University of Kentucky has remained dedicated to academic excellence.

Commonwealth Stadium

Courtesy of University of Kentucky Media Relations Office

KENTUCKY

Q. In what year did the nickname *Wildcats* become official?

A. 1911.

———— 🏈 ————

Q. Who set a new Kentucky game record in 1969 for most consecutive forward pass completions?

A. Bernie Scruggs (11 passes).

———— 🏈 ————

Q. What 1911–13 Kentucky player later gained fame with the St. Louis Browns for pitching the first home run ball to Babe Ruth?

A. Jim Park.

———— 🏈 ————

Q. What trophy, introduced during the 1925 season, is held by the winning team after each Kentucky–Tennessee contest?

A. The Ice Water Barrel (actually a whiskey barrel).

———— 🏈 ————

Q. Dedicated September 2, 1993, what facility serves as the indoor practice field for the Wildcats?

A. Nutter Field House.

———— 🏈 ————

Q. What Kentucky coach was relieved of his responsibilities during the 1926 season, only to have the players go on strike and force his return?

A. Fred J. Murphy.

———— 🏈 ————

Q. In what year did Kentucky participate in its first nationally televised game?

A. 1956, against Georgia Tech.

KENTUCKY

Q. The playing field of the University of Kentucky was officially given what name in 1908?

A. Stoll Field.

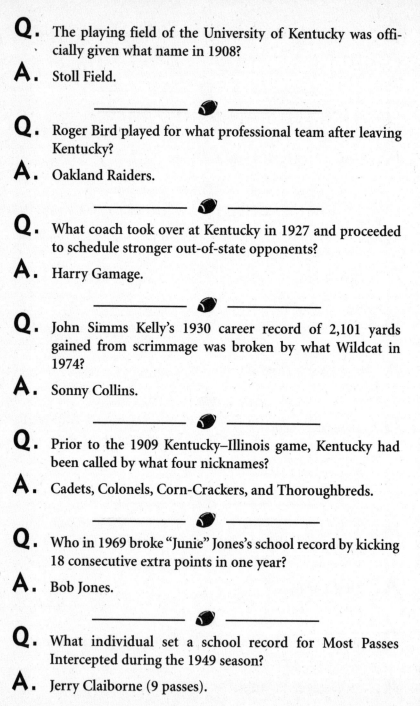

Q. Roger Bird played for what professional team after leaving Kentucky?

A. Oakland Raiders.

Q. What coach took over at Kentucky in 1927 and proceeded to schedule stronger out-of-state opponents?

A. Harry Gamage.

Q. John Simms Kelly's 1930 career record of 2,101 yards gained from scrimmage was broken by what Wildcat in 1974?

A. Sonny Collins.

Q. Prior to the 1909 Kentucky–Illinois game, Kentucky had been called by what four nicknames?

A. Cadets, Colonels, Corn-Crackers, and Thoroughbreds.

Q. Who in 1969 broke "Junie" Jones's school record by kicking 18 consecutive extra points in one year?

A. Bob Jones.

Q. What individual set a school record for Most Passes Intercepted during the 1949 season?

A. Jerry Claiborne (9 passes).

Q. During his college career of 1933, 1934, and 1935, quarterback Norris McMillan was known by what nickname?

A. "OO."

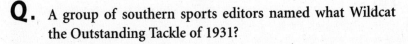

Q. A group of southern sports editors named what Wildcat the Outstanding Tackle of 1931?

A. Ralph "Babe" Wright.

Q. During the 1956 season what Wildcat was listed on 14 of the 21 first-team All-American teams?

A. Lou Michaels.

Q. Completed in 1973 what stadium replaced Stoll Field?

A. Commonwealth Stadium.

Q. As the youngest full-time starter in Division 1-A football, what 17-year-old Wildcat was named Freshman All-American for the 1999 season?

A. Kip Sixbery.

Q. During the 1985 season what starter led Kentucky in rushing, receiving, kickoff returns, and all-purpose running?

A. Marc Logan.

Q. What individual is credited with bringing football to the University of Kentucky?

A. Professor A. M. Miller.

Q. The Wildcats scored their first win against what opponent in 43 years with a 21–13 victory in 1939?

A. Vanderbilt.

———————— 🏈 ————————

Q. What nickname was given to 1986 senior quarterback Bill Ransdell by his teammates?

A. "Dollar Bill," because he was always on the money.

———————— 🏈 ————————

Q. What 1931–33 Kentucky player put on kicking exhibitions before the games, ending with a kick through the goal posts and into the crowd from 75 yards distance?

A. Ralph Kercheval.

———————— 🏈 ————————

Q. After completion of his Kentucky football career, Rick Kestner signed to play with what professional team?

A. Baltimore Colts.

———————— 🏈 ————————

Q. Taking the helm in 1934, what Kentucky football coach was the first Notre Dame graduate to coach a Kentucky athletic team?

A. Chet Wynne.

———————— 🏈 ————————

Q. What Wildcat quarterback was the No. 1 NFL draft pick in 1999?

A. Tim Couch.

———————— 🏈 ————————

Q. A new Kentucky individual career record for most points by a kicker was set by what 1974–76 letterman?

A. John Pierce (130 points).

Q. What Lexington drugstore was the favorite hangout for Wildcat fans during the 1920s?

A. Casey Jones's Drug Store.

Q. Looking back on his 1924 senior year, what legendary Kentucky fullback said he couldn't remember a game in which he wasn't knocked unconscious?

A. Curtis M. Sanders.

Q. What Kentucky quarterback came within one yard in 1965 of tying Zeke Bratkowski's SEC passing record of 1,824 yards set in 1952?

A. Rick Norton.

Q. In 1950 Babe Parilli set an all-time national collegiate record for most passes in one season with how many touchdowns?

A. Twenty-three.

Q. What assistant coach at Kentucky replaced Hal Mumme in 2001 as head football coach?

A. Guy Morriss.

Q. The University of Kentucky Athlete of the Year award went to what defensive end in 1984?

A. Keith Martin.

Q. What 5' 10", 145-pound Wildcat scored a touchdown within the first five minutes of his first game, played in 1939?

A. Ermal Allen.

Q. What individual set the school's season record for Most Total Tackles in 1985?

A. Larry Smith (152 tackles).

Q. Who followed Blanton Collier as head football coach of Kentucky in 1962?

A. Charlie Bradshaw.

Q. Kentucky met what opponent in the 1950 Orange Bowl?

A. Santa Clara.

Q. Coach Jerry Claiborne was born in what Kentucky town?

A. Hopkinsville.

Q. Prior to accepting the head football coaching position at Kentucky, A. D. Kirwan coached at what two Louisville high schools?

A. Male High and Manual High.

Q. What is the playing surface in Commonwealth Stadium?

A. Bermuda grass.

Q. How many yards did Wildcat Mark Higgs rush during the 1987 season?

A. 1,278.

Q. The Rodes brothers, J. W. and Pete, of Kentucky's pre-World War I teams were called by what nicknames?

A. "Black Doc" and "Red Doc."

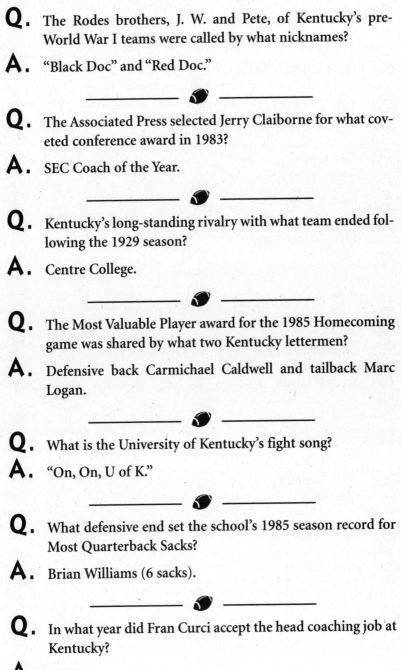

Q. The Associated Press selected Jerry Claiborne for what coveted conference award in 1983?

A. SEC Coach of the Year.

Q. Kentucky's long-standing rivalry with what team ended following the 1929 season?

A. Centre College.

Q. The Most Valuable Player award for the 1985 Homecoming game was shared by what two Kentucky lettermen?

A. Defensive back Carmichael Caldwell and tailback Marc Logan.

Q. What is the University of Kentucky's fight song?

A. "On, On, U of K."

Q. What defensive end set the school's 1985 season record for Most Quarterback Sacks?

A. Brian Williams (6 sacks).

Q. In what year did Fran Curci accept the head coaching job at Kentucky?

A. 1973.

KENTUCKY

Q. In what year did Kentucky play its first night game?

A. 1929.

———— 🏈 ————

Q. Where was former Wildcat Head Football Coach Hal Mumme born on March 29, 1952?

A. San Antonio, Texas.

———— 🏈 ————

Q. For what professional football team did Kentucky's flamboyant "Shipwreck" Kelly play?

A. The old Brooklyn Dodgers.

———— 🏈 ————

Q. What Kentucky All-SEC sophomore quarterback of 1958 joined the Wildcat coaching staff in 1982?

A. Jerry Eisaman.

———— 🏈 ————

Q. What Wildcat was chosen for the NCAA Top Five Student-Athlete award in 1978?

A. Linebacker Jim Kovach.

———— 🏈 ————

Q. Who defeated Kentucky in the 1999 Outback Bowl?

A. Penn State (26–14).

———— 🏈 ————

Q. Whom did "Bear" Bryant choose as team manager in 1946?

A. Frank Sadler.

Q. In what bowl did Kentucky play its first post-season game?

A. Great Lakes Bowl (1947).

Q. What Wildcat, who later became famous in the NFL for his placekicking, kicked only one field goal during his Kentucky career?

A. George Blanda.

Q. During what year did Kentucky call upon ringers to complete its football squad?

A. 1903.

Q. A touchdown by what opponent in the closing seconds of the 1993 Peach Bowl plunged the Wildcats into a 14–13 loss?

A. Clemson.

Q. In 1954 and 1955 Bob Hardy received All-SEC honors playing what postion?

A. Quarterback.

Q. The Jones twins, Harry and Larry, who played at Kentucky from 1950 to 1952, wore what numbers on their jerseys?

A. 1A and 1B.

Q. What Kentucky football coach received the SEC Coach of the Year award in his first season at the school?

A. Blanton Collier (1954).

KENTUCKY

Q. What 1960–62 letterman set the Kentucky individual career record for Most Passes Caught?

A. Tom Hutchinson (94 passes).

--- 🏈 ---

Q. Charlie Bradshaw's 1962 team was known by what nickname?

A. The "Thin Thirty."

--- 🏈 ---

Q. What Kentucky back was selected to All-SEC honors in 1933, the first year the conference was organized?

A. Ralph Kercheval.

--- 🏈 ---

Q. Kentucky lost to West Virginia in what post-season classic?

A. The 1983 Hall of Fame Bowl.

--- 🏈 ---

Q. What Ashland native became Kentucky's first All-American?

A. Clyde Johnson.

--- 🏈 ---

Q. Kentucky named what sophomore tailback its Most Outstanding Player of the 1984 Hall of Fame Bowl?

A. Marc Logan.

--- 🏈 ---

Q. Charlie Bradshaw earned his first of four football letters at what position in 1946?

A. Center.

Q. Who served as head football coach at Kentucky from 1990 through 1995?

A. Bill Curry.

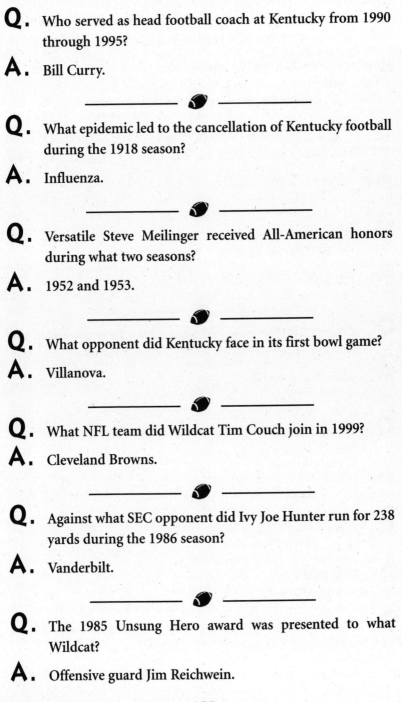

Q. What epidemic led to the cancellation of Kentucky football during the 1918 season?

A. Influenza.

Q. Versatile Steve Meilinger received All-American honors during what two seasons?

A. 1952 and 1953.

Q. What opponent did Kentucky face in its first bowl game?

A. Villanova.

Q. What NFL team did Wildcat Tim Couch join in 1999?

A. Cleveland Browns.

Q. Against what SEC opponent did Ivy Joe Hunter run for 238 yards during the 1986 season?

A. Vanderbilt.

Q. The 1985 Unsung Hero award was presented to what Wildcat?

A. Offensive guard Jim Reichwein.

Q. After Alabama's victory over the Wildcats in 1936, what Kentucky linebacker gained great praise from Tide coach Frank Thomas?

A. Gene Myers.

———— 🏈 ————

Q. A. D. Kirwan, who later went on to coach Kentucky, starred at halfback and end for the Wildcats during which seasons?

A. 1923, 1924, and 1925.

———— 🏈 ————

Q. What Wildcat was named Outstanding Defensive Player of the 1977 Japan Bowl?

A. Art Still.

———— 🏈 ————

Q. Coach "Bear" Bryant said what Kentucky quarterback was the best fake-and-throw passer he had ever seen?

A. Vito "Babe" Parilli.

———— 🏈 ————

Q. How many catches did Wildcat receiver James Whalen make during the 1999 season?

A. Ninety.

———— 🏈 ————

Q. With a 13–7 victory in the 1951 Sugar Bowl, Kentucky shattered the 31-game winning streak for what opponent?

A. Oklahoma.

———— 🏈 ————

Q. What Wildcat became the first sophomore since Harry Gilmer to be named SEC Player of the Year in 1973?

A. Sonny Collins.

Q. Don Phelps, noted as possibly the best running back to play for Coach Bryant at Kentucky, played three years for what professional team?

A. Cleveland Browns.

Q. What Kentucky tackle was named Most Valuable Player of the 1951 Sugar Bowl?

A. Walt Yowarsky.

Q. Coach Jerry Claiborne was a member of what Kentucky bowl team?

A. 1950 Orange Bowl team.

Q. In 1946 what Kentucky end became the first player in the SEC to make the all-conference list in football and basketball?

A. Wallace "Wah Wah" Jones.

Q. In what year did the Kentucky football team first begin to travel by air?

A. 1946.

Q. What Kentucky lineman of the 1916 squad later became governor of the state and a member of the U.S. Senate?

A. Earle Clements.

Q. What Wildcat assistant coach under Coach Blanton Collier later bacame the highly successful coach of the Baltimore Colts and Miami Dolphins?

A. Don Shula.

Q. During the 1995 season Wildcat Moe Williams rushed what impressive number of yards?

A. Sixteen hundred.

———— 🏈 ————

Q. Kentucky met what opponent in the 1952 Cotton Bowl?

A. Texas Christian.

———— 🏈 ————

Q. Paul "Bear" Bryant's coaching career at Kentucky resulted in what record?

A. 60–23–5.

———— 🏈 ————

Q. What Kentucky football coach of the 1915–16 seasons was born on the Vanderbilt campus and later became the president of the University of Florida?

A. Dr. John J. Tigert.

———— 🏈 ————

Q. During the 1987 season what team did the Wildcats defeat 41–0?

A. Utah State.

———— 🏈 ————

Q. Of what capable Kentucky quarterback did Coach Bryant say he was like a cow on ice?

A. Steve Meilinger.

———— 🏈 ————

Q. Due to lax 1906 rules and World War I, J. White Guyn, Eger Murphee, and John Heber each received how many football letters from the University of Kentucky?

A. Five.

Q. In the 1999 HomePoint.com Music City Bowl, who defeated Kentucky 20–13?

A. Syracuse.

───────── 🏈 ─────────

Q. How many years did John Ray serve as head football coach of Kentucky?

A. Four: 1969–72.

───────── 🏈 ─────────

Q. In what year did Coach Bryant lead Kentucky to the SEC football championship?

A. 1950.

───────── 🏈 ─────────

Q. What Kentucky star of the 1915 victory over Purdue was the first Kentucky pilot to die in World War I in 1918?

A. Howard Kinne.

───────── 🏈 ─────────

Q. By what score did Kentucky defeat Wisconsin in the 1984 Hall of Fame Bowl?

A. 20–19.

───────── 🏈 ─────────

Q. The unconventional coaching style of Hal Mumme, including such plays as the "Air Raid" and the "Go For It," was given what nickname?

A. "Mummeball."

───────── 🏈 ─────────

Q. During the unforgettable 1949 season, what two Wildcats received All-SEC honors?

A. Center Harry Ulinski and tackle Bob Gain.

Q. The gallant efforts of the 1898 team rendered them what nickname?

A. "The Immortals."

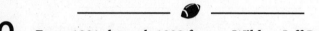

Q. From 1991 through 1999 former Wildcat Jeff Brady played for how many different NFL teams?

A. Seven.

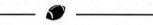

Q. What head football coach first inaugurated spring practice at Kentucky?

A. E. R. Sweetland.

Q. For how many games did "Bear" Bryant utilize his new jersey numbering system in 1953?

A. Two.

Q. What school did Kentucky defeat 21–0 in the 1976 Peach Bowl game?

A. North Carolina.

Q. Coach "Ab" Kirwan instituted what system of play?

A. The two-platoon system.

Q. What Kentucky player of 1949 and 1950 went on to become the highly successful head coach of LSU?

A. Charles McClendon.

KENTUCKY

Q. At the beginning of the twentieth century, the Board of Trustees at Kentucky appropriated how much annually to secure the continuation of football at the school?

A. $150.

━━━━━━━━ 🏈 ━━━━━━━━

Q. What Wildcat went on to play in the NFL from 1988 to 1995 with the Cowboys, Eagles, Dolphins, and the Cardinals?

A. Mark Higgs.

━━━━━━━━ 🏈 ━━━━━━━━

Q. What Wildcat was the "Iron Man" on the 1962 squad?

A. Herschel Turner.

━━━━━━━━ 🏈 ━━━━━━━━

Q. What Wildcat was named Outstanding Back of the 1952 Cotton Bowl?

A. "Babe" Parilli.

━━━━━━━━ 🏈 ━━━━━━━━

Q. What is the middle name of Hal Mumme, who served as head football coach at Kentucky from 1997 to 2000?

A. Clay.

━━━━━━━━ 🏈 ━━━━━━━━

Q. During the 1894 season what 1893 Purdue tackle did Kentucky hire as trainer, while actually planning to play him against Centre College?

A. W. P. Finney.

━━━━━━━━ 🏈 ━━━━━━━━

Q. What 1952 Kentucky defensive guard was a sophomore selection to the All-Time Cotton Bowl team?

A. Ray Correll.

KENTUCKY

Q. What Wildcat ran a 100-yard touchdown play on a kickoff return against Florida in 1998?

A. Craig Yeast.

Q. During what years was Paul "Bear" Bryant head football coach at Kentucky?

A. 1946–1953.

Q. What 1955 and 1965 Kentucky All-Americans attended Flaget High School in Louisville?

A. End Howard Schnellenberger and quarterback Rick Norton.

Q. In what season was Kentucky, lineman Bob Gain labeled "best in the nation"?

A. 1950.

Q. During his career at Kentucky, Tim Couch set 14 SEC records and how many school records?

A. Twenty-six.

Q. Who represented Kentucky in the 1978 Canadian–American Game?

A. Defensive tackle James Ramey.

LOUISIANA STATE

Federal land grants in the early 1800s laid the groundwork for the Louisiana State University. In 1853, by action of the Louisiana General Assembly, the Seminary of Learning was created. On January 2, 1860, the institution officially opened its doors near Pineville with then Col. William Tecumseh Sherman serving as superintendent. Nineteen cadets comprised the student body on opening day, and the faculty consisted of five professors. At its opening the name Louisiana State Seminary of Learning and Military Academy was given to the new school. With the outbreak of the Civil War, Colonel Sherman resigned, and most of the student body disbanded for enlistment.

On July 31, 1861, the Seminary closed. On April 1, 1862, the school reopened for a year, but closed again on April 23, 1863, following the invasion of Union forces. Some property, including the library, was destroyed by federal troops under General Smith, but General Sherman intervened to save the main structure. Following the end of the Civil War, the seminary reopened only to have the main building burn in 1869. The seminary moved to Baton Rouge where classes were held in the facilities of the Institute for the Deaf, Dumb, and Blind. In March 1870 the Seminary was renamed Louisiana State University. State aid to the university was suspended in 1872, resulting in many of the cadets being sent home. Enrollment continued to decline and the class of 1873 was the last class to graduate until after reconstruction.

LOUISIANA STATE

The Louisiana State Agricultural & Mechanical College opened at the University of Louisiana facilities in New Orleans in 1874. The following year the new school's title changed to Louisiana A&M College, and the institution was racially integrated. The reconstruction ended in 1876, and the state legislature combined Louisiana State University and Louisiana A&M College. In 1882 LSU conferred bachelor degrees for the first time in nine years.

Stability came to the university in the late 1800s and early 1900s, and with stability came growth. Construction of the present campus began in 1922 with the first classes being held in the new facilities in 1926. The end of World War II saw a boom in enrollment that continued through the remainder of the twentieth century. Today LSU stands as one of the leading centers of academia in the nation.

Tiger Stadium

Courtesy of Louisiana State University Sports Information

Q. Since the beginning of football at LSU, in what year did the university not field a team?

A. 1918, due to World War I.

———————— 🏈 ————————

Q. What LSU football coach was the first to have his own statewide television show?

A. Paul Dietzel.

———————— 🏈 ————————

Q. What Caribbean school did LSU play and defeat 56–0 on Chirstmas Day in 1907?

A. Havana University.

———————— 🏈 ————————

Q. Who organized LSU's first football team?

A. Professor Charles E. Coates.

———————— 🏈 ————————

Q. What is the playing surface of Tiger Stadium?

A. Natural grass.

———————— 🏈 ————————

Q. What Louisiana governor took a major interest in promoting the LSU football program in 1928?

A. Huey P. Long.

———————— 🏈 ————————

Q. John Garlington, LSU's 1967 All-American defensive end, played with what NFL team from 1968 to 1977?

A. Cleveland Browns.

Q. What was LSU's slogan for the 1946 game with Alabama?

A. "Beat Bama for Bernie."

———— 🏈 ————

Q. On what date did LSU play its first football game?

A. November 25, 1893.

———— 🏈 ————

Q. What LSU assistant replaced "Biff" Jones as head football coach in December of 1934?

A. Bernie Moore.

———— 🏈 ————

Q. What accurate prediction was painted on a large sign mysteriously placed at Tulane Stadium prior to the 1949 game with LSU?

A. LSU 21–TU 0.

———— 🏈 ————

Q. LSU's Ken Konz was a longtime star with what NFL team?

A. Cleveland Browns.

———— 🏈 ————

Q. Ken Kavanaugh Jr. played at LSU during what seasons?

A. 1969–71.

———— 🏈 ————

Q. In 1987–89 what LSU Tiger received Academic All-SEC honors a quarter of a century after his father, White Graves, received the same honor?

A. Sol Graves.

Q. By what nicknames are the LSU football team known?

A. "Tigers" and "Fighting Tigers."

———— 🏈 ————

Q. Whom did Governor Huey P. Long install as football coach at LSU in 1932?

A. Lawrence M. "Biff" Jones.

———— 🏈 ————

Q. What great LSU quarterback led the 1908 team to a 10–0 season?

A. George Ellwood "Doc" Fenton.

———— 🏈 ————

Q. Who did Coach Gaynell Tinsley say was probably the best all-around LSU player he ever coached?

A. Abner Wimberly.

———— 🏈 ————

Q. What outstanding award was presented to Billy Cannon at the close of the 1959 season?

A. The Heisman Memorial Trophy.

———— 🏈 ————

Q. During the 1946 game with Tulane, what LSU halfback had punt returns of 92 and 94 yards called back?

A. Jim Cason.

———— 🏈 ————

Q. LSU players and fans accused Vanderbilt of what during a 1902 game, leading to a general brawl?

A. Signal stealing by spying.

LOUISIANA STATE

Q. What year marked LSU's first undefeated season?

A. 1895.

───────── 🏈 ─────────

Q. On what date did LSU play its first Sugar Bowl game?

A. New Year's Day 1936.

───────── 🏈 ─────────

Q. What was the length of Bill Pitcher's 1924 record LSU punt?

A. Ninety-three yards (73 in the air).

───────── 🏈 ─────────

Q. The scoreless 1947 Cotton Bowl standoff between LSU and Arkansas received what title due to adverse weather conditions?

A. The "Ice Bowl."

───────── 🏈 ─────────

Q. Who coached the 1894 and 1895 LSU football teams?

A. A. P. Simmons.

───────── 🏈 ─────────

Q. The Fighting Tigers met and defeated the Fighting Irish in what 1997 bowl game?

A. Independence Bowl (27–9).

───────── 🏈 ─────────

Q. In what years did NFL superstar runner Steve VanBuren play for LSU?

A. 1941–43.

LOUISIANA STATE

Q. What was LSU's opponent in the 1926 game in which both teams hit the crossbar with point-after-touchdown kicks?

A. Mississippi State.

———— 🏈 ————

Q. During the 1977 season how many consecutive touchdown passes were caught by Carlos Carson?

A. Six (five against Rice and one against Florida).

———— 🏈 ————

Q. What governor of Louisiana called the LSU football team into his office for a pep talk in 1925?

A. Henry Fuqua.

———— 🏈 ————

Q. In what seasons did Bernie H. Moore coach LSU football?

A. 1935–47.

———— 🏈 ————

Q. Against what college team did LSU first play?

A. Tulane.

———— 🏈 ————

Q. Academic All-American honors were bestowed upon what two LSU players in 1971?

A. Jay Michaelson and Tommy Butaud.

———— 🏈 ————

Q. For what annual salary was Mike Donahue hired as coach in 1923?

A. $10,000.

Q. What player scored four touchdowns in LSU's 28–7 victory over Holy Cross in 1939?

A. Ken Kavanaugh Sr.

Q. Who coached the LSU football team during the 1904–06 seasons?

A. D. A. Killian.

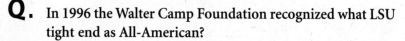

Q. In 1996 the Walter Camp Foundation recognized what LSU tight end as All-American?

A. David LaFleur.

Q. Dalton Hilliard set an LSU record by rushing for how many yards during the 1982–85 seasons?

A. 4,050.

Q. Against what opponent did Sen. Huey P. Long organize a special train convoy to transport 3,200 fans to a 1934 game?

A. Vanderbilt.

Q. What four seasons did Mike Archer serve as head football coach at LSU?

A. 1987–90.

Q. What epidemic in the south severely curtailed LSU's 1897 and 1898 seasons?

A. Yellow fever.

Q. Who was LSU's greatest quarterback of the 1940s?

A. Y. A. Tittle.

———— 🏈 ————

Q. For how many yards did LSU's Harvey Williams rush during the 1987 season?

A. 1,001.

———— 🏈 ————

Q. How many years did Jerry Stovall coach at LSU?

A. Four: 1980–83.

———— 🏈 ————

Q. What organization ruled in favor of LSU in the controversial 1901 game with Tulane?

A. Southern Intercollegiate Athletic Association.

———— 🏈 ————

Q. At the October 31, 1959, game against Ole Miss, what LSU player received the tag of "the Halloween Ghost"?

A. Billy Cannon.

———— 🏈 ————

Q. Who was the captain of the 1893 LSU team who later became governor of Louisiana?

A. R. G. Pleasant.

———— 🏈 ————

Q. In the 1944 game against Rice, what was the length of Ray Coates's legendary punt?

A. Seventy-six yards.

Q. What school was LSU's only collegiate victim during the 1903 season?

A. Louisiana Tech.

Q. Following the 1943 Orange Bowl, what transportation did Lewis Gottlieb purchase in Miami so the LSU team could return home?

A. Several used cars.

Q. What coach took over the LSU football team in 1911?

A. J. K. Dwyer.

Q. In LSU's first 29 football seasons, how many different people served as coach?

A. Sixteen.

Q. What LSU swimming coach in 1936 was the first to publicly suggest that LSU should have a live tiger mascot?

A. W. G. "Hickey" Higginbotham.

Q. The *Nashville Banner* bestowed what honor on Coach Bill Arnsparger in 1984?

A. SEC Coach of the Year.

Q. During the 1906 game against the Monroe Athletic Club, who became the first LSU player to throw a forward pass?

A. Halfback J. C. Muller.

Q. Billy Cannon rushed for how many yards during his LSU career?

A. 1,867.

Q. What was the first season that Charles McClendon served as head football coach at LSU?

A. 1962.

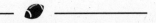

Q. President William H. Taft was present at what 1909 LSU game in New Orleans?

A. LSU vs. Sewanee.

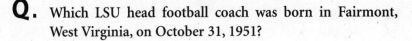

Q. How many yards did Eddie Kennison gain for LSU on punt returns during his 1993–95 collegiate career?

A. 947.

Q. Which LSU head football coach was born in Fairmont, West Virginia, on October 31, 1951?

A. Nick Lou Saban.

Q. LSU dedicated its new playing field in the 1917 season opener against what team?

A. Southwestern Louisiana.

Q. In a 34–0 loss LSU became one of five schools defeated in six days by what school in 1899?

A. Sewanee.

Q. On October 8, 1988, with 1:41 left on the clock, vibrations from the thunderous explosion of excitement over the Tigers' come-from-behind touchdown against Auburn registered on what piece of equipment in LSU's Geology Department?

A. Seismograph.

———— 🏈 ————

Q. What player received the school's first Most Valuable Player trophy at the end of the 1927 season?

A. Lola T. "Babe" Godfrey.

———— 🏈 ————

Q. What LSU player was inducted into the Louisiana Sports Hall of Fame in 1981?

A. Jerry Stovall.

———— 🏈 ————

Q. Who followed Bernie Moore as head football coach at LSU?

A. Gaynell Tinsley.

———— 🏈 ————

Q. Against what traveling show did Sen. Huey P. Long wage battle to insure good attendance at the 1934 LSU–SMU game?

A. The Barnum & Bailey Circus.

———— 🏈 ————

Q. What was LSU kicker David Brown's field goal percentage for the 1989 season?

A. 100 percent (14 of 14).

———— 🏈 ————

Q. Over what school did LSU score its first victory?

A. Centenary (1894).

LOUISIANA STATE

Q. What LSU football coach was fired mid-season 1916?

A. E. T. McDonnell.

———————— 🏈 ————————

Q. In 1941 against Tennessee what kicker set an LSU record for most yards punted in a game?

A. Leo Bird (519 yards).

———————— 🏈 ————————

Q. Against what team did LSU play the 1949 "wet field" game?

A. North Carolina.

———————— 🏈 ————————

Q. What amount was raised to purchase LSU's first mascot tiger in 1936?

A. $750.

———————— 🏈 ————————

Q. What was the final score in LSU's largest ever lopsided win against Southwestern Louisiana in 1936?

A. 93–0.

———————— 🏈 ————————

Q. What opponents did LSU tie during the 1906 season?

A. Mississippi State and Arkansas.

———————— 🏈 ————————

Q. In 1998 what LSU noseguard received All-American honors from the Associated Press and the *Football News*?

A. Anthony McFarland.

Q. What 1942 LSU halfback later played professional baseball and managed the Oakland As to a 1974 World Championship?

A. Alvin Dark.

Q. Who coached LSU to the 27–6 upset victory over Tulane in 1919?

A. Irving R. Pray.

Q. What school dealt LSU a one-point heartbreaker loss at the 1983 Orange Bowl?

A. Nebraska.

Q. How many points did LSU's Tom Dutton score against Tulane in 1912?

A. Thirty-four.

Q. What was the jersey number of Billy Cannon?

A. Twenty.

Q. LSU defeated what school 10–7 in the 1996 Peach Bowl?

A. Clemson.

Q. In whose honor was LSU's first live mascot tiger named on October 21, 1936?

A. Football trainer Mike Chamber.

LOUISIANA STATE

Q. Who coached LSU's 1908 undefeated team?

A. Edgar R. Wingard.

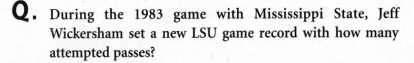

Q. During the 1983 game with Mississippi State, Jeff Wickersham set a new LSU game record with how many attempted passes?

A. Fifty-one.

Q. Where did Nick Lou Saban serve as head football coach prior to coming to LSU in 2000?

A. Michigan State.

Q. In what city did LSU play its first game?

A. New Orleans, at Sportsman's Park.

Q. What name was given to the victory flag created in 1939 to be presented to the winning school at LSU and Tulane gridiron confrontations?

A. "The Rag."

Q. How many points did Kevin Faulk score during his 1995–98 career at LSU?

A. 318.

Q. What was Paul Dietzel's first official act as LSU's head football coach?

A. He fired assistant Coach Will Walls.

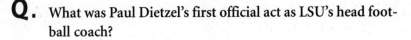

LOUISIANA STATE

Q. What LSU player scored two touchdowns in the 1922 game against Tulane?

A. Roland Kizer.

Q. LSU's 500th win was against what school in 1982?

A. Kentucky (34–10).

Q. Who made the spectacular 90-yard off-tackle run during the 1936 LSU victory over Auburn at Birmingham?

A. Guy Milner.

Q. Due to a bitter cold wave, how many fans came to Tiger Stadium to see LSU play Oregon on December 17, 1932?

A. Around two hundred.

Q. The 1949 LSU team was given what nickname?

A. The "Cinderella team."

Q. What two LSU players have received the Walter Camp Memorial Trophy?

A. Billy Cannon (1959) and Jerry Stovall (1962).

Q. What LSU quarterback attempted 1,005 passes during his career?

A. Jeff Wickersham.

Q. How many times did LSU fumble the ball during the 1936 game with Texas at Austin?

A. Ten.

_____ 🏈 _____

Q. Who broke "Doc" Fenton's long-standing LSU field goal distance record with a 46-yard kick in the 1965 opening game?

A. Doug Moreau.

_____ 🏈 _____

Q. What malady affected both teams at the 1932 matchup between LSU and Tulane?

A. Influenza.

_____ 🏈 _____

Q. In what three seasons did LSU defeat Tulane with a final score of 62–0?

A. 1958, 1961, and 1965.

_____ 🏈 _____

Q. Jack Torrance, who played for LSU during the 1931–33 seasons, later set a world record in what track and field event?

A. Shot put.

_____ 🏈 _____

Q. What was the nickname of LSU's early 1920s spectacular punter Clarence Ives?

A. "Fatty."

_____ 🏈 _____

Q. In what year did the LSU team first fly to an away game?

A. 1939 (to Boston).

LOUISIANA STATE

Q. Into what three teams was the exciting 1958 football squad divided?

A. The White, Gold (or "Go"), and the Chinese Bandits.

———————— 🏈 ————————

Q. Who holds the LSU career record for most punts during the twentieth century?

A. Chad Kessler (186 punts).

———————— 🏈 ————————

Q. In what year was the first game in Tiger Stadium played?

A. 1924.

———————— 🏈 ————————

Q. Before a sellout crowd in Shreveport, what team did LSU defeat 45–26 in the 1995 Independence Bowl?

A. Michigan State.

———————— 🏈 ————————

Q. Who made three spectacular touchdown runs against Spring Hill in 1931?

A. Art Foley.

———————— 🏈 ————————

Q. How many touchdowns did Charles Alexander score in the 1977 season?

A. Seventeen.

———————— 🏈 ————————

Q. What Texas coach was borrowed for the last few LSU games of the 1916 season?

A. Dana X. Bible.

LOUISIANA STATE

Q. What are LSU's colors?

A. Purple and gold.

Q. Who became the first All-SEC player from LSU in 1933?

A. Jack Torrance.

Q. In 1959 who did LSU play in the first game nationally televised from Tiger Stadium?

A. Rice.

Q. Who preceded Gerry DiNardo as head football coach at LSU?

A. Curley Hallman.

Q. What 1944–47 LSU player went on to be affiliated with the Redskins, Lions, 49ers, Eagles, Packers, and Cardinals?

A. Dan Sandifer.

Q. In the 1965 Sugar Bowl, Billy Ezell and Pat Screen quarterbacked LSU to a come-from-behind 13–10 victory over what team?

A. Syracuse.

Q. By what name was Head Coach Charlie McClendon called by his players?

A. "Coach Mac."

Q. What independent powerhouse did LSU defeat in 1971?

A. Notre Dame (28–2).

———————— 🏈 ————————

Q. In what year did Coach Bernie Moore rule that only unmarried men could play for LSU (except players returning from the previous season)?

A. 1937.

———————— 🏈 ————————

Q. What was the price of admission to LSU's first game?

A. Fifty cents.

———————— 🏈 ————————

Q. What happened to the river steamer *Royal* on which the 1894 LSU team traveled to play the Natchez Athletic Club?

A. It ran aground on a sandbar.

———————— 🏈 ————————

Q. What group provided the halftime entertainment during the 1934 game against Oregon at Baton Rouge?

A. Captain Claire Chennault and an army flying team.

———————— 🏈 ————————

Q. In 1952 who set an LSU season record for most punts?

A. Al Doggett (81 points).

———————— 🏈 ————————

Q. Against what team did Harvey Williams suffer a severe knee injury during the 1987 season?

A. Tulane.

MISSISSIPPI

CHAPTER EIGHT

The University of Mississippi was chartered by the Mississippi legislature in 1844. The legislature appointed a committee to recommend a site for the new institute of higher learning. The two leading contenders were the coastal community of Mississippi City and the small hamlet of Oxford in the rolling hills of northern Mississippi. By a one-vote margin Oxford was chosen, and in 1848 the University of Mississippi opened its doors with eighty students enrolled.

On January 9, 1861, the State of Mississippi adopted an Ordinance of Secession written by University of Mississippi mathematics professor L.Q.C. Lamar. Against the pleadings of the university chancellor and Confederate President Jefferson Davis, many of the students withdrew from classes and enlisted in the army. By fall the campus was deserted. During the next few years warring armies criss-crossed the university's campus, and the future of the institution was in doubt. In the fall of 1865, following the surrender at Appomattox, 163 students, three faculty members, and the chancellor returned to the campus. The university faced several more difficult years, but hard work and tenacity paid off with the creation of a great center of academic excellence.

The University of Mississippi has a rich collection of traditions, one of which is its nickname, "Ole Miss." In 1896 a contest was held to name the new student yearbook. The name Ole Miss, suggested by Elma Meek of Oxford, was selected for the publication. Through the years the name slowly became synonymous with the university.

Another tradition is the nickname for the university's athletic teams, the Rebels. The title came about in 1936 via a contest sponsored by *The Mississippian* student newspaper. Over 200 names were proposed. With the list narrowed, the top five suggestions were presented to 42 newsmen, 18 of whom voted for Rebels suggested by Judge Ben Guider of Vicksburg. Today Ole Miss and the Rebels are rich in excellence and tradition.

Vaught-Hemingway Stadium   Courtesy of University of Mississippi Sports Information

MISSISSIPPI

Q. During what season did Mississippi win its first Southeastern Conference championship?

A. 1947.

Q. Who was the leading Ole Miss receiver in 1986?

A. J. R. Ambrose (32 receptions).

Q. What Ole Miss kicker scored the only point of his college career during the 1925 victory over A&M (Mississippi State)?

A. Webb Burke.

Q. Who organized Mississippi's first football team?

A. Professor Alexander Lee Boudurant.

Q. All-SEC lineman-guard Jimmy "Tank" Crawford maintained what hobby while on the Ole Miss campus?

A. Beekeeping.

Q. Who in 1936 became the first Ole Miss player to receive All-American honors?

A. Frank M. Kinard.

Q. The annual gridiron confrontation between Mississippi and what rival is known as the "Egg Bowl"?

A. Mississippi State.

MISSISSIPPI

Q. What was Coach John Howard "Johnny" Vaught's career record at Ole Miss?

A. 190–61–12.

———————— 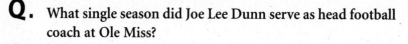 ————————

Q. Who captained the 1895 Mississippi team?

A. Ewell D. Scales.

———————— 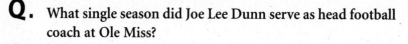 ————————

Q. Although he was drafted by the Washington Redskins, with what team did Mississippi's Charley Conerly actually start his professional playing career?

A. New York Giants.

———————— 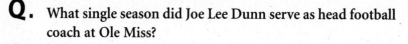 ————————

Q. How many times did Ole Miss fumble during the 1964 Sugar Bowl game with Alabama?

A. Eleven.

———————— 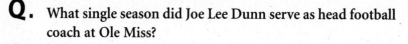 ————————

Q. What single season did Joe Lee Dunn serve as head football coach at Ole Miss?

A. 1994.

———————— 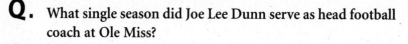 ————————

Q. During the 1910 season, what two schools did Mississippi defeat 16–0?

A. Tulane and Alabama.

———————— 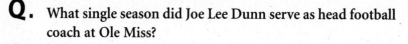 ————————

Q. What was the nickname of the 1921 team captain Howard D. Robinson?

A. "Santa Claus."

MISSISSIPPI

Q. In an almost two-to-one victory, who did Ole Miss defeat 35–18 in the 1998 Independence Bowl?

A. Texas Tech.

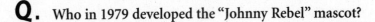

Q. Who in 1979 developed the "Johnny Rebel" mascot?

A. Cheerleader Jeff Hubbard.

Q. What 135-pound 1918 scrub went on to captain the 1922 team?

A. Calvin Barbour.

Q. Of his 52 attempts, how many passes did Archie Manning complete during the 1969 game with Alabama?

A. Thirty-three.

Q. What was Billy Brewer's first season as head football coach at Ole Miss?

A. 1983.

Q. What two Mississippi players were invited to play in the first North-South All-Star game in 1932?

A. Tom Swayze and Guy Turnbow.

Q. How many seasons did Steve Sloan serve as head coach at Ole Miss?

A. Five: 1978–82.

Q. What 1894 team captain later became a state supreme court justice in Mississippi?

A. William Henry Cook.

Q. During the 1930 season the Ole Miss football team was called by what nickname?

A. The "Flood."

Q. What former Auburn football captain coached Ole Miss for part of the 1901 and all of the 1902 seasons?

A. Dan Martin.

Q. In 1997 what Rebel set a new Mississippi record for most passes in a season?

A. Stewart Patridge (352 passes).

Q. Against what team did Ole Miss play the inaugural game in Mississippi Memorial Stadium in 1953?

A. Chattanooga.

Q. What former Ole Miss player began his NFL career with the Buffalo Bills in 1976?

A. Ben Williams.

Q. What nickname was used to describe the 1927 Ole Miss football team?

A. The "Mighty Mississippians."

MISSISSIPPI

Q. Who was head football coach at Ole Miss from 1974–77?

A. Ken Cooper.

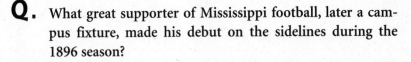

Q. What great supporter of Mississippi football, later a campus fixture, made his debut on the sidelines during the 1896 season?

A. Blind Jim Ivy.

Q. How many school and SEC records did Archie Manning establish during his three-year career at Ole Miss?

A. Thirty-six (Ole Miss) and seven (SEC).

Q. What incident led to five Ole Miss players refusing to participate in the 1900 game with Alabama?

A. A fraternity fight.

Q. Ole Miss center Richard L. "Wimpy" Winther played for what two NFL teams?

A. Green Bay Packers and New Orleans Saints.

Q. In what year was the grass playing surface reinstalled in the campus stadium at Ole Miss?

A. 1984.

Q. To what two teams did Mississippi lose during the 1906 season?

A. Vanderbilt and Sewanee.

Q. What was the first Ole Miss game televised in color?

A. 1960 Sugar Bowl.

Q. What assistant football coach at the University of Pennsylvania became head coach at Ole Miss in 1909?

A. Dr. Nathan P. Stauffer.

Q. During his 1993–96 seasons at Old Miss, Ta'Boris Fisher set a school career record with how many passes caught?

A. 139.

Q. What were the total gate receipts at Mississippi's first confrontation with Alabama on October 27, 1894?

A. $180.

Q. What are the Ole Miss colors?

A. Cardinal red and navy blue.

Q. During his 1971 and 1972 seasons at Ole Miss, how many touchdown passes did Burney Veazey catch?

A. Twelve.

Q. What were the only two schools played by Mississippi in 1905?

A. Cumberland and A&M (Mississippi State).

Q. During his 1989–92 collegiate career at Ole Miss, how many points did Brian Lee score?

A. 207.

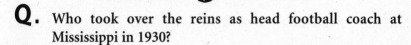

Q. Who took over the reins as head football coach at Mississippi in 1930?

A. Ed Lee Walker.

Q. What was the final score in Mississippi's 1954 romp over Villanova at Philadelphia's Municipal Stadium?

A. 52–0.

Q. Ole Miss All-American Freddie Joe Nunn, 1984, played for what NFL team?

A. St. Louis Cardinals.

Q. What was the distance of Jack Burke's record kickoff return that put Ole Miss on the scoreboard in the 1931 contest with Alabama?

A. 109 yards.

Q. How many teeth did Mississippi's Barney Poole lose due to an elbow to the mouth during the 1948 game with Tulane?

A. Eight.

Q. What was the only school to defeat Mississippi during its brilliant 1959–63 winning streak?

A. LSU.

Q. What Ole Miss tackle gained first-team All-American recognition in 1954?

A. Rex Reed Boggan.

———— 🏈 ————

Q. What is the full name of Mississippi's amazing quarterback Archie Manning?

A. Elisha Archibald Manning III.

———— 🏈 ————

Q. Where was Homer Hazel a two-time All-American before coming to coach football at Mississippi in 1925?

A. Rutgers.

———— 🏈 ————

Q. Where was Ole Miss Coach David Nelson Cutcliffe born on September 16, 1954?

A. Birmingham, Alabama.

———— 🏈 ————

Q. What great Ole Miss tackle of the 1935–37 seasons was known by the nickname "Bruiser"?

A. Frank Kinard.

———— 🏈 ————

Q. What lopsided win did Mississippi score over Southwestern Baptist University in 1904?

A. 114–0.

———— 🏈 ————

Q. What two Ole Miss players teamed up for an 83-yard pass and run play during the 1961 game with Houston?

A. Glynn Griffing and Chuck Morris.

Q. What 1987 freshman set an Ole Miss record with one interception per game in seven straight games?

A. Todd Sandroni.

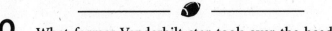

Q. What former Vanderbilt star took over the head football coaching position at Ole Miss in 1915?

A. Fred Robbins.

Q. Of all the years Mississippi has fielded a football team, in what year did the team have no official coach?

A. 1905.

Q. In Mississippi's last game of the twentieth century, what team did the Rebels defeat 27–25 in the Independence Bowl, December 31, 1999?

A. Oklahoma.

Q. First-team All-American honors were awarded to what two Ole Miss players in 1959?

A. Charles Flowers and Marvin Terrell.

Q. How many times has Ole Miss had back-to-back SEC championship seasons?

A. Twice: 1954–55 and 1962–63.

Q. What 1933–35 Ole Miss player was known as the "Tupelo Ghost"?

A. Rab Rodgers.

MISSISSIPPI

Q. At what two colleges did Billy Brewer serve as head coach before coming to Ole Miss?

A. Southeastern Louisiana and Louisiana Tech.

───────── 🏈 ─────────

Q. When did Mississippi play its first intercollegiate game?

A. November 11, 1893.

───────── 🏈 ─────────

Q. What was the first season for two-platoon football at Ole Miss?

A. 1949.

───────── 🏈 ─────────

Q. Prior to the 1961 game with LSU, Ole Miss players received a Louisiana-postmarked package containing a large assortment of what type of apparel?

A. Panties.

───────── 🏈 ─────────

Q. What was the first bowl game in which Ole Miss participated?

A. The Orange Bowl (January 1, 1936).

───────── 🏈 ─────────

Q. Who was the first football coach to serve consecutive seasons at Ole Miss?

A. Mike Harvey (1903–04).

───────── 🏈 ─────────

Q. How many consecutive points-after-touchdown did Mississippi's Jimmy Keyes score?

A. Forty (1965–67).

MISSISSIPPI

Q. In 1921 where did Ole Miss play its first post-season game?

A. Havana, Cuba, in Almendares Park.

———————— 🏈 ————————

Q. In the 1991 Gator Bowl, what team gave Mississippi a 35–3 trouncing?

A. Michigan.

———————— 🏈 ————————

Q. During what seasons did John Howard "Johnny" Vaught coach at Ole Miss?

A. 1947–70 and part of 1973.

———————— 🏈 ————————

Q. By what nickname was Charley Conerly known during his Ole Miss career?

A. "Roach."

———————— 🏈 ————————

Q. During the 1984 season Jon Howard set an Ole Miss record with how many field goals?

A. Thirteen.

———————— 🏈 ————————

Q. Who in 1975 became the first black Ole Miss player to receive first-team All-American honors?

A. Ben Williams.

———————— 🏈 ————————

Q. What was the final score of the Ole Miss 1971 Peach Bowl win over Georgia Tech?

A. 41–18.

Q. Where did Harry Mehre coach immediately prior to joining Ole Miss for the 1938 season?

A. University of Georgia.

———————— 🏈 ————————

Q. In the 1999 season what Rebel gained 652 yards on kickoff returns?

A. Deyce McAllister.

———————— 🏈 ————————

Q. What late 1920s Ole Miss player was noted for taping his ears back and never wearing a helmet when he played?

A. C. M. "Tadpole" Smith.

———————— 🏈 ————————

Q. In what 1989 bowl game did Mississippi defeat Air Force 42–29?

A. Liberty Bowl.

———————— 🏈 ————————

Q. Who became the first Mississippi player to score a touchdown during intercollegiate play?

A. Garland Mordecai Jones (1893).

———————— 🏈 ————————

Q. What was the jersey number of Mississippi's great All-SEC and All-American player Charley Conerly?

A. Forty-two.

———————— 🏈 ————————

Q. Who was Ole Miss's opponent in the 1986 Independence Bowl?

A. Texas Tech.

Q. How many yards did John Dottley rush during the 1949 season?

A. 1,312.

———————— 🏈 ————————

Q. Who started the 1901 season as coach for the Ole Miss football team?

A. William Sibley.

———————— 🏈 ————————

Q. In preseason listings what magazine selected Ole Miss as the top college team in the nation in 1954?

A. *Collier's.*

———————— 🏈 ————————

Q. What Mississippi quarterback was unanimously selected as Most Outstanding Player of the 1958 Sugar Bowl game?

A. Ray Brown.

———————— 🏈 ————————

Q. Who set an Ole Miss season record in 1980 by catching nine touchdown passes?

A. Ken Toler.

———————— 🏈 ————————

Q. What was Dr. Nathan P. Stauffer's coaching record while at Mississippi from 1909–11?

A. 17–7–2.

———————— 🏈 ————————

Q. With what NFL team did Allen Green sign after his career at Ole Miss?

A. Dallas Cowboys.

Q. In 1995 LeMay Thomas tied Floyd Franks's 1969 Ole Miss record with how many pass receptions?

A. Fifty-six.

Q. Who was the 6'1", 220-pound star left tackle of the 1909–11 Ole Miss teams?

A. Fred Carter.

Q. How many points did Carl Edward "Hoppy" Langley III score during his 1976–79 career at Ole Miss?

A. 178.

Q. From what school did Coach Harold "Red" Drew borrow uniforms for the Ole Miss team in 1946?

A. University of Alabama.

Q. Coach Vaught listed what 1969 game as his "most emotional game ever"?

A. Ole Miss vs. Alabama.

Q. How many kickoff returns did Rick Kimbrough make during the 1974 Ole Miss game with Alabama?

A. Six.

Q. The 1928 backfield of "Tadpole" Smith, "Cowboy" Woodruff, "Doodle" Rushing, Reuben Wilcox, and Gerald Walker were known by what nickname?

A. The "Flying Five."

Q. Who scored an Ole Miss kicking record with 59 points during the 1987 season?

A. Bryan Owen.

Q. What star senior of the 1938 Ole Miss team was nicknamed "Bullet"?

A. Parker Hall.

Q. In what year did Ole Miss set the team record for most fumbles?

A. 1949 (53 fumbles).

Q. Mississippi's great quarterback Jerry D. "Jake" Gibbs played for what professional baseball team after finishing at Ole Miss?

A. New York Yankees.

Q. In the 1927 win over Florida, what Ole Miss player did not wear a jersey?

A. Austin "Ap" Applewhite.

Q. Over what team was Ole Miss victorious in its first Cotton Bowl appearance in 1956?

A. Texas Christian (14–13).

Q. What seasons did Bill Driver serve as football coach at Mississippi?

A. 1913 and 1914.

Q. How many penalties were called against Ole Miss during the 1949 game with TCU?

A. Nineteen.

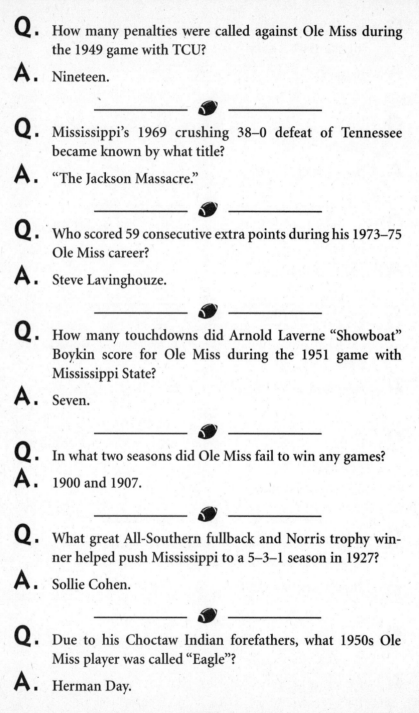

Q. Mississippi's 1969 crushing 38–0 defeat of Tennessee became known by what title?

A. "The Jackson Massacre."

Q. Who scored 59 consecutive extra points during his 1973–75 Ole Miss career?

A. Steve Lavinghouze.

Q. How many touchdowns did Arnold Laverne "Showboat" Boykin score for Ole Miss during the 1951 game with Mississippi State?

A. Seven.

Q. In what two seasons did Ole Miss fail to win any games?

A. 1900 and 1907.

Q. What great All-Southern fullback and Norris trophy winner helped push Mississippi to a 5–3–1 season in 1927?

A. Sollie Cohen.

Q. Due to his Choctaw Indian forefathers, what 1950s Ole Miss player was called "Eagle"?

A. Herman Day.

Q. Against what team did Mississippi play its first intercollegiate game?

A. Southwestern Baptist University (1893).

———— 🏈 ————

Q. From 1939–41 what touchdown duo was known as the "H" boys?

A. John A. "Junie" Hovious and Merle Hapes.

———— 🏈 ————

Q. In 1982 what player set an Ole Miss record for most passes completed during a single game with 37 completions against Tennessee?

A. Kent Austin.

———— 🏈 ————

Q. What two Ole Miss kickers share the school record of 74 punts for a season?

A. Greg Breland (1974) and Jim Miller (1978).

———— 🏈 ————

Q. In what bowl game did Ole Miss participate on January 1, 1948?

A. The first Delta Bowl.

———— 🏈 ————

Q. What Ole Miss player dropkicked four field goals during the 1910 game between Mississippi and Henderson Brown?

A. Billy Cahall.

———— 🏈 ————

Q. What 1918 Ole Miss quarterback from Clarksdale, Mississippi, was called "Alphabet"?

A. A. B. Carney.

Q. What Ole Miss player led the SEC in scoring during the 1949 season?

A. John "Kayo" Dottley (84 points).

———————— 🏈 ————————

Q. Against what school did Mississippi play its first bowl game?

A. Catholic University (1936 Orange Bowl).

———————— 🏈 ————————

Q. What Ole Miss player was selected by Coach Vaught in 1948 to become the first Split-T quarterback in southern football?

A. Farley "Fish" Salmon.

———————— 🏈 ————————

Q. What Ole Miss player set a school season record in 1980 for most offensive plays?

A. John Fourcade (411).

———————— 🏈 ————————

Q. Who commuted between Memphis and Oxford on weekends to coach the first Ole Miss team?

A. J. W. S. Rhea.

———————— 🏈 ————————

Q. Against what team during the 1914 season did Ole Miss quarterback Pete Deal pick up a fumble and run 99 yards for a touchdown?

A. LSU.

———————— 🏈 ————————

Q. During the 1949 season how many interceptions did Bobby Wilson make?

A. Ten.

MISSISSIPPI STATE

CHAPTER NINE

Mississippi State University began as the Agricultural and Mechanical College of the State of Mississippi. This institution was one of the land-grant colleges established under the Morrill Act of 1862. The college was officially chartered by the Mississippi legislature on February 28, 1878, "to fulfill the mission of offering training in agriculture, horticulture, and the mechanical arts . . . without excluding other scientific and classical studies, including military tactics." The first students were received at the new school in the fall of 1880 with Gen. Stephen D. Lee serving as college president.

In 1887 the United States Congress passed the Hatch Act, and under its guidelines the following year the state was able to establish the Agricultural Experiment Station in conjunction with the college. Two additional pieces of federal legislation proved of great value to A&M College. The Smith-Lever Act of 1914 paved the way for agriculture and home economics extension offices in every county in the state. Also the Smith-Hughes Act of 1917 provided for the training of vocational education teachers. In both areas A&M College was able to broaden its mission and service to the state.

Several new fields of study were introduced to the college in the early 1900s: the College of Engineering (1902), the College of Agriculture (1903), the School of Industrial Pedagogy (1909), the School of General Science (1911), the College of Business and Industry (1915), the Mississippi Agricultural

Extension Service (1915), and the Division of Continuing Education (1919). In 1931 the Mississippi Legislature changed the name of A&M College to Mississippi College. This new name would remain until 1958, when the school was renamed Mississippi State University.

Davis Wade Stadium at Scott Field

Courtesy of Mississippi State University Athletic Media Relations

Q. In 1901 Mississippi A&M won its first collegiate victory over what opponent?

A. Ole Miss (17–0).

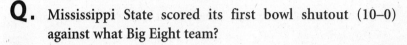

Q. Mississippi State scored its first bowl shutout (10–0) against what Big Eight team?

A. The Kansas Jayhawks (1981).

Q. W. J. "Blondy" Williams refused to wear what piece of equipment during his A&M career (1909–12)?

A. A helmet.

Q. During his 1952 and 1953 seasons at Mississippi State, how many points did Jackie Parker score?

A. 185.

Q. In what year did Mississippi A&M officially adopt the bulldog as its mascot?

A. 1905.

Q. What are the school colors of Mississippi State?

A. Maroon and white.

Q. Following the cancellation of football in 1897, what A&M professor rallied support and gained acceptance of the sport in 1901?

A. Irwin Dancy Sessums.

Q. After defeating Bob Neyland's Vols 7–0 in 1950, what Maroon coach received National Coach of the Week honors?

A. Arthur "Slick" Morton.

———————— 🏈 ————————

Q. In what year did the Bulldogs earn a trip to the Liberty Bowl?

A. 1963.

———————— 🏈 ————————

Q. What building serves as the Bulldogs main indoor practice and conditioning facility?

A. Shira Fieldhouse Complex.

———————— 🏈 ————————

Q. Quarterback Billy Stacy played for what NFL team?

A. St. Louis Cardinals.

———————— 🏈 ————————

Q. Mississippi A&M met what opponent in its first football game?

A. Southwestern Baptist University.

———————— 🏈 ————————

Q. In 1935 Mississippi State hired what well-respected motivational football coach known as "the Major"?

A. Ralph Irvin Sasse.

———————— 🏈 ————————

Q. What kicker set a Mississippi State record with an 84-yard punt during the 1974 game against Alabama?

A. Mike Patrick.

MISSISSIPPI STATE

Q. Who became Mississippi State's first All-American football player?

A. Erwin "Buddy" Elrod.

Q. Mississippi State played its first major post-season game in what bowl?

A. The Orange Bowl.

Q. Linebacker Jonie Cooks made first-team All-SEC during what two seasons?

A. 1980 and 1981.

Q. Known for being a "dude" of an athlete, what 1912–15 letterman was called "Dudy"?

A. C. R. Noble.

Q. During the 1930 season Coach "Red" Cagle ordered what change in uniforms, hoping to break "the Maroon jinx"?

A. White jerseys.

Q. On December 28, 1974, Mississippi State faced North Carolina in what bowl?

A. The Sun Bowl.

Q. Scott Field was named for what A&M football letterman and track star?

A. Col. Don Scott.

MISSISSIPPI STATE

Q. What Mississippi State football coach later became the famous Silver Fox of Minnesota?

A. Bernie Bierman.

———————— 🏈 ————————

Q. Following his college football career, Kinney Jordan signed with what professional team?

A. Tampa Bay Buccaneers.

———————— 🏈 ————————

Q. In 1952 and 1953 what Maroon quarterback was named the SEC Most Valuable Player?

A. Jackie Parker.

———————— 🏈 ————————

Q. In the 1999 Cotton Bowl, what team defeated State 38–11?

A. Texas.

———————— 🏈 ————————

Q. "Blondy" Black was a native of what Mississippi town?

A. Philadelphia.

———————— 🏈 ————————

Q. Who was selected State's second All-American in 1944?

A. Tom "Shorty" McWilliams.

———————— 🏈 ————————

Q. Coach Bob Tyler led his teams to how many bowl contests?

A. One (the 1974 Sun Bowl).

MISSISSIPPI STATE

Q. Mississippi State's favorite live mascot, purchased in 1925, was given what name?

A. "Bully."

Q. On November 16, 1895, who selected the school's colors?

A. W. M. Matthews, first team captain, manager, quarterback, and coach.

Q. In 1970 what head coach led the Bulldogs to their first winning season (6–5) since 1963?

A. Charles Shira.

Q. Facing freezing temperatures State defeated what opponent in Philadelphia's 1963 Liberty Bowl?

A. North Carolina State.

Q. Head Football Coach Paul Davis was a graduate of what SEC school?

A. Ole Miss.

Q. What nickname was given to Coach Dan Martin's 1903 team?

A. "Boss Team."

Q. Who captained the history-making 1935 team?

A. Willie Stone.

MISSISSIPPI STATE

Q. Who did Mississippi State play in the 2000 Sanford Independence Bowl?

A. Texas A&M.

———— 🏈 ————

Q. Brothers Harper Davis (1945–48) and Arthur Davis (1953–55) played what position during their careers at State?

A. Halfback.

———— 🏈 ————

Q. Mississippi A&M played its first football game in what year?

A. 1895.

———— 🏈 ————

Q. The 1909 game against Tulane in New Orleans was halted for 15 minutes to give recognition to what unexpected special guest?

A. President William Howard Taft.

———— 🏈 ————

Q. At the 1905 Alabama game in Tuscaloosa, what A&M quarterback threw the school's first forward pass?

A. Hal McGeorge.

———— 🏈 ————

Q. Due to lack of finances, A&M football withdrew from the Southern Intercollegiate Athletic Association in 1922 and joined what smaller conference?

A. The Southern Conference.

———— 🏈 ————

Q. In 2000 what Bulldog became the third quarterback in the school's history to pass for at least ten touchdowns in back-to-back seasons?

A. Wayne Madkin.

Q. A&M forfeited a 1904 game against what school due to a disagreement with the referee?

A. Alabama.

Q. Because of poor field conditions, what name was given to the 1907 A&M vs. Ole Miss game played in Jackson?

A. "Battle of Lake Jackson."

Q. Coach Jackie Sherrill, who became head football coach at Mississippi State in 1991, was born in what Oklahoma town on November 28, 1943?

A. Duncan.

Q. Against what 1910 opponent did A&M win by its greatest margin of victory?

A. Howard University (82–0).

Q. Athletic Director C. R. Noble hired what head football coach in the spring of 1954?

A. Darrell Royal.

Q. What Mississippi State center was named to All-American honors in 1960?

A. Tom Goode.

Q. In what place of honor was State's long-time mascot "Bully I" laid to rest in 1939 after being struck by a bus on campus?

A. Scott Field's 50-yard line.

Q. During what year did Mississippi A&M football produce its first undefeated season?

A. 1903.

———— 🏈 ————

Q. What 1930s kicker holds the Mississippi State record for most punts during a single game?

A. Bob Hardison (16 against Texas Christian).

———— 🏈 ————

Q. Where was Coach Chadwick's 1911 team invited to play on New Year's Day?

A. Havana, Cuba.

———— 🏈 ————

Q. Letterman Rockey Felker quarterbacked for Mississippi State during what seasons?

A. 1972–74.

———— 🏈 ————

Q. Who was the Bulldogs' first four-sport letterman?

A. Morley Jennings.

———— 🏈 ————

Q. To what team did Mississippi State fall victim in the 1995 Peach Bowl Game?

A. North Carolina State.

———— 🏈 ————

Q. "Blondy" Black averaged how many yards per carry in his 1940–42 varsity seasons?

A. 6.1.

Q. As a result of a childhood foot infection, what Maroon quarterback wore a size 12 shoe on one foot and a size 11 on the other?

A. Jackie Parker.

———— 🏈 ————

Q. On October 1, 1904, A&M lost to Vanderbilt by what final score?

A. 61–0.

———— 🏈 ————

Q. Showing great skill as an athlete, who became the second Bulldog to letter in four sports?

A. C. R. Noble.

———— 🏈 ————

Q. Who set a new MSU single game record with 5.5 sacks in the November 30, 1996, game against Mississippi?

A. Greg Favors.

———— 🏈 ————

Q. How many seasons was Coach Emory Bellard at the helm of Mississippi State football?

A. Seven: 1979–85.

———— 🏈 ————

Q. Numerically, where did Rockey Felker rank in the number of head coaches who have served Mississippi State?

A. Twenty-ninth.

———— 🏈 ————

Q. Who became the captain of Coach W. D. Chadwick's first team?

A. DeWitt W. Billingsley.

Q. Mississipi State earned a bid to what bowl in 1981?

A. The Hall of Fame Bowl.

Q. Against what school did A&M score a 75–0 victory in 1907?

A. Mercer.

Q. After his 1952 graduation Joe Fortunato began a notable career with what professional team?

A. Chicago Bears.

Q. Which Bulldog, with a total of 27 touchdowns, holds the MSU career touchdown record?

A. Michael Davis.

Q. A&M letterman Leo Seal Sr. (1909–10) was a native of what community?

A. Logtown.

Q. Who became State's first black football player?

A. Frank Dowsing (1970–72).

Q. The running pass was introduced to A&M by what head coach?

A. Fred Holtcamp.

MISSISSIPPI STATE

Q. A&M and Mississippi College played to what final score in 1913?

A. 1–0.

———— 🏈 ————

Q. All-American Jackie Parker set a 1952 SEC scoring record with how many points?

A. 120.

———— 🏈 ————

Q. The 1908 school yearbook was speaking of what athlete when it observed he was the "first Yankee to be elected captain at A&M"?

A. H. B. "Little" Furman.

———— 🏈 ————

Q. On December 14, 1951, who was named head football coach, replacing "Slick" Morton?

A. Murray Warmath.

———— 🏈 ————

Q. During the 1942 Duquesne game, "Blondy" Black faked a punt in his end zone and ran how many yards for a touchdown?

A. 107.

———— 🏈 ————

Q. What Starkville native captained the victorious 1940 squad?

A. Hunter Corhern.

———— 🏈 ————

Q. Prior to the 1935 Army game, what good luck charm was given to Coach Ralph Sasse?

A. An Irish Free State Penny.

Q. During the McKeen era what player made first-team All-SEC four years?

A. "Shorty" McWilliams.

———— 🏈 ————

Q. Who defeated Mississippi State 21–17 in the 1993 Peach Bowl?

A. North Carolina.

———— 🏈 ————

Q. When was the first night game played at Scott Field?

A. October 28, 1933.

———— 🏈 ————

Q. In 1907 who became A&M's first full-time coach?

A. Fred Furman.

———— 🏈 ————

Q. On October 22, 1994, what Bulldog shattered MSU's single game passing record with 466 yards against Tulane?

A. Derrick Taite.

———— 🏈 ————

Q. For whom was the new 1905 A&M playing field named?

A. President of A&M Jack Hardy (Hardy Field).

———— 🏈 ————

Q. In 1942 Coach Allyn McKeen gave a football scholarship to what young Texas boy who later chose to play for his home state?

A. Tom Landry.

MISSISSIPPI STATE

Q. What 1940 Bulldog tailbacks were known as the "J" boys?

A. Harvey Johnson and Billy Jefferson.

———— 🏈 ————

Q. Following the 1957 season what coach was named by the *Nashville Banner* as SEC Coach of the Year?

A. Wade Walker.

———— 🏈 ————

Q. What great honor was bestowed on quarterback Jackie Parker by the Canadian Football League in the 1960s?

A. Canadian Football League Player of the Decade.

———— 🏈 ————

Q. When did MSU defeat Alabama for the first time at Scott Field?

A. November 26, 1996.

———— 🏈 ————

Q. Ralph Sasse ended his three-year coaching career (1935–37) at State with what record?

A. 20–10–2.

———— 🏈 ————

Q. Bulldog games played in Jackson are held at what stadium?

A. Mississippi Memorial Stadium.

———— 🏈 ————

Q. What game is considered to be Mississippi State's greatest football victory?

A. The 1935 13–7 upset of Army.

Q. During the 1974 bout with Memphis State, who set a Maroon record for most yards gained by a freshman in one game?

A. Dennis Johnson (198).

————  ————

Q. In what year did Mississippi State join the Southeastern Conference?

A. 1933, the first year of its organization.

————  ————

Q. In what two seasons did A&M's sharp defensive unit shut out seven teams?

A. 1910 and 1913.

————  ————

Q. A&M played a limited schedule through 1918 due to what epidemic?

A. Influenza.

————  ————

Q. What Bulldog kicker set a school record with five field goals during the 1998 matchup with Arkansas?

A. Brian Hazelwood.

————  ————

Q. What Maroon receiver set a Mississippi State game record with 14 pass receptions against Mississippi in 1969?

A. David Smith.

————  ————

Q. Who was named Most Valuable Offensive Player of the 1974 Sun Bowl?

A. Terry Vitrano.

Q. Who kicked the game-winning point for the Bulldogs against the Haskell Indians in 1917?

A. Substitute quarterback Bob Sanders.

———— 🏈 ————

Q. Defensive back Frank Dowsing received first-team All-American honors in what year?

A. 1972.

———— 🏈 ————

Q. Playing at A&M from 1904 to 1907, quarterback Hal McGeorge was given what nickname by his teammates?

A. "Bottle."

———— 🏈 ————

Q. In 1938 a player revolt led to the dismissal of what coach?

A. Dr. Emerson "Spike" Nelson.

———— 🏈 ————

Q. What admission was charged to see Alabama and Mississippi A&M in 1906?

A. 25¢.

———— 🏈 ————

Q. Mississippi State was represented at the 1982 Olympia Gold Bowl in San Diego by what Bulldog defensive tackle?

A. Glen Collins.

———— 🏈 ————

Q. What was the relationship of 1908 team captain Harry "Little" Furman to coach Fred Furman?

A. Brother.

Q. What Maroon quarterback set an SEC career record for Most Yards Gained Rushing during his 1980–83 tenure at State?

A. John Bond (2,280).

———————— 🏈 ————————

Q. In the 1914 61–0 victory over Tulane, an assistant coach raised what charge against A&M regarding its clothing?

A. He said their trousers had been greased.

———————— 🏈 ————————

Q. In the third annual Liberty Bowl in Memphis, who defeated MSU 38–15 on December 29, 1991?

A. Air Force.

———————— 🏈 ————————

Q. In 1993 what Bulldog kicker set a MSU single season record with 17 field goals?

A. Tom Burke.

———————— 🏈 ————————

Q. Letterman Morley Jennings (1910–11) was known by what nickname?

A. "Topsy."

———————— 🏈 ————————

Q. During the 1941 Orange Bowl, what two Bulldogs scored the touchdowns in the 14–7 win over Georgetown?

A. John "Spic" Tripson and "Big" Billy Jefferson.

———————— 🏈 ————————

Q. What turn-of-the-century A&M football player was the only three-time captain in the school's history?

A. Hal McGeorge (1905–07).

Q. Coach McKeen named what back as the best runner in the history of Maroon football?

A. J. T. "Blondy" Black.

———— 🏈 ————

Q. For the first time in the school's history, what year did Mississippi State beat both Auburn and Alabama on the road?

A. 1997.

———— 🏈 ————

Q. What A&M football player scored seven touchdowns during the 1914 game against Cumberland?

A. Harry McArthur.

———— 🏈 ————

Q. What State quarterback won the 1941 SEC championship by pulling a 38-yard sneak against Ole Miss?

A. Jennings Moates.

———— 🏈 ————

Q. The 1926 season produced what trophy to be held each year by the winner of the A&M and Ole Miss game?

A. The Golden Egg.

———— 🏈 ————

Q. From 1989–92 which Bulldog carried the pigskin 1,332 yards for a MSU career record on punt return yardage?

A. Tony Jones.

———— 🏈 ————

Q. During the 1970 game with LSU, who set a Maroon record for Most Pass Attempts during a game?

A. Joe Reed with 53 attempts.

MISSISSIPPI STATE

Q. During the 1913 game against Mississippi College, what opposing coach forfeited the game with eight minutes to go?

A. Dana X. Bible.

———— 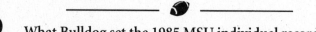 ————

Q. What Bulldog set the 1985 MSU individual record for most passes completed in one game?

A. Don Smith (22 passes).

———— 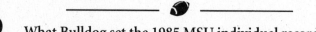 ————

Q. All-American defensive tackle Jimmy Webb was selected for what honor following the 1974 Sun Bowl?

A. Most Valuable Defensive Player.

———— 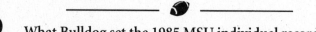 ————

Q. Coach Ralph Sasse promised quarterback Ike Pickle what prize if he would win the 1935 Alabama game?

A. Coach Sasse's gray trousers and gray suede shoes.

———— 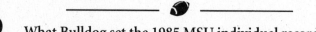 ————

Q. In 1988 Tony Shell set a Maroon record with how many attempted passes for that season?

A. 335.

———— 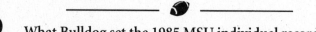 ————

Q. During the 1978 game with Tennessee, who set a Maroon record for most consecutive completed passes in a game?

A. Dave Marler (11 passes).

———— 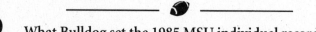 ————

Q. Coach Allyn McKeen's nine seasons at Mississippi State resulted in what outstanding career record?

A. 65–19–3.

SOUTH CAROLINA

CHAPTER TEN

The University of South Carolina was chartered by the state legislature in 1801 as South Carolina College. This institution became the first public university to be continuously supported by annual state appropriations. The college quickly gained a reputation for academic excellence and was soon known as one of the most distinguished institutions in the United States. The early 1800s faculty included noted writer Francis Lieber, nationally known scientists John and Joseph LeConte, and chemist William Eller, who invented the first daguerreotype in the nation. Many great judicial, political, and business leaders graduated from South Carolina College during the antebellum era.

With the outbreak of the Civil War, the student body volunteered for service in the Army of the Confederacy, which brought about the closing of the school in June 1862. The campus buildings were used by the Confederate government as hospital facilities. By the time General Sherman's federal forces reached Columbia in February 1865, wounded Union soldiers were being treated on campus. Fire raged through Columbia, but federal troops helped save the campus buildings from being destroyed.

From the time the school reopened in 1865 through the end of the nineteenth century, the college went through a rechartering, six reorganizations, and several name changes. Bureaucratic, economic, and political chaos seemed the order of the day. In 1906 the school was rechartered for the third time as the University of South Carolina. During the next two decades, the school's mission was redefined, and its academic energies rechanneled. The university developed an institutional objective to furnish both liberal and professional education to the people of South Carolina and the nation. The university survived the Great Depression, World War II, Civil Rights unrest, Viet Nam, and a myriad of other social and political issues during the twentieth century. Today the University of South Carolina once again stands at the forefront of higher education.

Williams-Brice Stadium   Courtesy of University of South Carolina Sports Information

Q. In what year did Gamecock George Rogers win the Heisman Trophy?

A. 1980.

———————— 🏈 ————————

Q. Having been called by such nicknames as Jaguars and Jackals, in what year did South Carolina's football team become known as the Gamecocks (originally Game Cocks)?

A. 1902.

———————— 🏈 ————————

Q. Five times during his 1986–89 career at USC, what Gamecock scored three touchdowns in a single game?

A. Harold Green.

———————— 🏈 ————————

Q. Who did the Gamecocks face off with on January 1, 2001, in the Outback Bowl?

A. Ohio State.

———————— 🏈 ————————

Q. To what school did South Carolina's first "unofficial" football team lose 44–0 on Christmas Eve 1892?

A. Furman.

———————— 🏈 ————————

Q. Gamecock Clyde "Mule" Bennett, who caught 34 passes during the 1952 season, later played five years with which NFL team?

A. Pittsburgh Steelers.

———————— 🏈 ————————

Q. Collin Mackie scored how many points in 1987 to secure the USC record for most points scored by a freshman during a single season?

A. 113.

Q. When USC played in the very first Gator Bowl (1946), what was the price for box seat tickets?

A. $4 each.

Q. In what year did a furor over counterfeit tickets lead to thousands of gate crashers filling up the sidelines at the Big Thursday game between USC and Clemson?

A. 1946.

Q. Which Gamecock was known as "The Cadillac" and "Steamboat Steve"?

A. Steve Wadiak.

Q. Who set a new USC record for most tackles in a season with 179 tackles in 1983?

A. Mike Durrah.

Q. Who defeated the Gamecocks 34–10 at the 1988 Liberty Bowl in Memphis?

A. Indiana.

Q. Who served as the "Voice of the Gamecocks" from 1952 until his retirement in 1995?

A. Bob Fulton.

Q. How many two-point conversions did the Gamecocks complete against Virginia on November 7, 1959?

A. Four.

Q. Who coached the 1896 and 1897 South Carolina teams?

A. R. S. Whaley.

Q. Gamecock Jamar Nesbit became a member of which NFL team in 1999?

A. Carolina Panthers.

Q. In 1986 and 1987, what Gamecock received a dozen national honors for his outstanding gridiron performance?

A. Sterling Sharpe.

Q. Who is the only USC head football coach to have been named Atlantic Coast Conference (ACC) Coach of the Year?

A. Paul Dietzel (1969).

Q. What early 1950s Gamecock was the first passer to surpass 2,000 career yards at USC?

A. Johnny Gramling.

Q. In 1999 what Gamecock received the honor of being named freshman All-American by the *Sporting News?*

A. Rashad Faison.

Q. In what year did South Carolina become a member of the Southeastern Conference?

A. 1992.

Q. What gridiron guru, outdoorsman, and sports writer, signed a five-year coaching contract with USC in 1920?

A. Sol Metzger.

Q. "Meatball" was the nickname of what All-Southern Conference center for USC in 1946?

A. Bryant Meeks Jr.

Q. On what date was the South Carolina—Clemson football rivalry born at Columbia's old fairgrounds off Elmwood Avenue?

A. November 13, 1896.

Q. How many times did the Gamecocks fumble the ball during the November 9, 1985, game with Florida State?

A. Eighteen.

Q. What Gamecock led the SEC in rushing in 1996?

A. Duce Staley.

Q. With South Carolina enrollment at 64 students, in what year was the school's first "official" football team fielded?

A. 1894.

Q. What lopsided defeat did South Carolina suffer at the hands of Clemson in 1900?

A. 51–0.

Q. What are USC's team colors?

A. Garnet and black.

———— 🏈 ————

Q. In 1972 what USC sports information director discovered and corrected the misnomer of South Carolina's 7–3 1903 season to the correct 8–2 win/loss ratio?

A. Tom Price.

———— 🏈 ————

Q. On October 8, 1966, Gamecock Bobby Bryant carried a punt return how many yards to score a touchdown against North Carolina State?

A. Ninety-eight yards.

———— 🏈 ————

Q. What USC coach authored *The Fighting Spirit* and *Winning Every Day*?

A. Lou Holtz.

———— 🏈 ————

Q. Gamecocks Dave "Junior" Cash '73, Bob Korn '53, John Letteup '72, Harold Lewis '55, and Percy Reeves '81 following graduation eventually entered what vocation?

A. Clergy.

———— 🏈 ————

Q. Who was South Carolina's team captain in the Gamecocks' 1902 12–6 victory over Clemson?

A. Thomas McCutcheon.

———— 🏈 ————

Q. In the 1995 season USC broke the record for most points scored in a season with how many points?

A. 401.

Q. What school did USC play in the 1910 season opener which set a "longest game" record by starting just past noon and lasting until almost sundown?

A. The College of Charleston.

———— 🏈 ————

Q. Branch Bocock, who served as the Gamecocks' football coach for the 1925–26 season was born in what Virginia community?

A. Woodstock.

———— 🏈 ————

Q. Aired over WIS-TV in Columbia, when was the first televised Gamecock home game?

A. November 7, 1953.

———— 🏈 ————

Q. In 1942 who became the first Gamecock to receive Associated Press All-American honors?

A. Louis Sossaman (center, second team).

———— 🏈 ————

Q. In 1912 what physician coached the Gamecocks to their first win over the Clemson Tigers in ten years?

A. Dr. Norman B. "Red" Edgerton.

———— 🏈 ————

Q. In the 1957 matchup with Texas, what Gamecock returned the opening kickoff 98 yards for a touchdown?

A. King Dixon.

———— 🏈 ————

Q. What USC football star was voted Player of the Year in the Southern Conference for the 1950 season?

A. Steve Wadiak.

SOUTH CAROLINA

Q. For the 1951 season Coach Rex Enright introduced what new formation?

A. The Vee.

————— 🏈 —————

Q. Which USC football coach inaugurated the use of closed-circuit television to enable the Gamecocks to better view their opponents' offensive and defensive lineups?

A. Warren Giese.

————— 🏈 —————

Q. Though the NCAA recognizes a 100-yard maximum, which Gamecock ran a kickoff return 104 yards against Duke for a touchdown on October 12, 1985?

A. Sterling Sharpe.

————— 🏈 —————

Q. Which two Gamecocks received ACC Player of the Year honors?

A. Alex Hawkins (1958) and Billy Gambrell (1962).

————— 🏈 —————

Q. Halfback Fritz Von Kolnitz, who helped carry South Carolina to a 5–2–1 season in 1912, later played for what professional baseball team?

A. Cincinnati Reds.

————— 🏈 —————

Q. What was the name of USC's original playing field?

A. Davis Field.

————— 🏈 —————

Q. During the 1988 matchup with East Carolina, USC's Todd Ellis's pass to what player set in motion a 97-yard touchdown?

A. Robert Brooks.

Q. What Gamecock quarterback recruit for the 1915 season later became chairman of USC's Board of Trustees?

A. Rut Osborne.

———— 🏈 ————

Q. Due to a scandal over the alleged hiring of "ringers" for the 1915 Gamecock team, USC forfeited games to what two schools?

A. Newberry and Presbyterian.

———— 🏈 ————

Q. USC threw how many touchdown passes against Kent during the October 7, 1995, game?

A. Six.

———— 🏈 ————

Q. In 1915 USC joined what collegiate sports organization?

A. Southern Intercollegiate Athletic Association (SIAA).

———— 🏈 ————

Q. What Gamecock kicked a 58-yard field goal against Georgia in the September 5, 1982, game?

A. Mark Fleetwood.

———— 🏈 ————

Q. In 1987 what national honor was bestowed on USC head Coach Joe Morrison?

A. Associated Press Southern Independent Coach of the Year.

———— 🏈 ————

Q. During his 1952–55 career at USC, Carl Brazell averaged how many yards per carry?

A. 5.7.

Q. For 1956, 1957, and 1958, which Gamecock was named Academic All-ACC?

A. King Dixon.

Q. What USC coach resigned following the dismal 1916 season that ended in a 3–6 win/loss record?

A. Rice Warren.

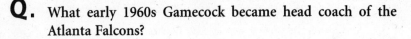

Q. What early 1960s Gamecock became head coach of the Atlanta Falcons?

A. Dan Reeves.

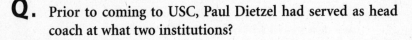

Q. Prior to coming to USC, Paul Dietzel had served as head coach at what two institutions?

A. LSU and West Point.

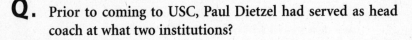

Q. What USC record number of interceptions did the Gamecocks have against Florida State during the November 10, 1984, game?

A. Seven.

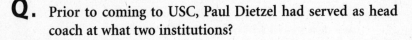

Q. What is the name of USC's mascot?

A. Cocky.

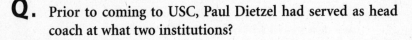

Q. Jay Feltz in 1979 and Chris Norman in 1983 each kicked what length of punts during regulation play, earning them recognition in the USC records?

A. Eighty-yard punts.

Q. Comprised of 22 cabooses, what unique tailgating facility is situated on the south side of Williams-Brice Stadium?

A. The Cockaboose Railroad.

Q. During the twentieth century what was the Gamecocks' worst losing season?

A. 1999 (0–11).

Q. From W. H. Whaley (1896) to Lou Holtz (2001), how many head coaches have served the Gamecocks?

A. Thirty-one.

Q. Against what school did South Carolina score its first victory in a 14–10 win on November 8, 1895?

A. Furman.

Q. In 1950 South Carolina's Steve Wadiak set a new Southern Conference rushing record with how many yards?

A. 998.

Q. Although W. Dixon Foster coached the Gamecocks during and after World War I, who replaced him during his hitch in the Navy for the 1918 season?

A. Frank Dobson.

Q. South Carolina quarterback Dan Reeves went on to become a star with what NFL team?

A. Dallas Cowboys.

Q. All-Southeastern Conference honors went to which Gamecocks for the 1997 season?

A. Boo Williams, Arturo Freeman, Jamar Nesbit, and Darren Hambrick.

Q. Following his time at USC, Bobby Bryant went on to distinguish himself with what professional team?

A. Minnesota Vikings.

Q. In 1967 what USC coach twisted one of his knees on the practice field, requiring surgery?

A. Paul Dietzel.

Q. Following the regular 1969 season, who did USC play in the second annual Peach Bowl in Atlanta?

A. West Virginia Mountaineers.

Q. What was the jersey number of Larry Suggs, who during his Gamecock career completed 355 passes out of 672?

A. Twelve.

Q. When was Carolina Stadium officially renamed Williams-Brice Stadium?

A. September 9, 1972.

Q. In 1919 the Gamecocks set a USC record for fewest points scored in nine games of play with what total for the season?

A. Twenty-five points.

Q. In the 1980–82 seasons what Gamecock had 26 quarterback sacks to set a USC career record?

A. Andrew Provence.

Q. In 1997 what Gamecock scored 10 touchdowns to set a USC record for most touchdowns during a season by a freshman?

A. Jermale Kelly.

Q. Who did South Carolina play in the 1975 Tangerine Bowl?

A. Miami (Ohio).

Q. Against Vanderbilt on October 21, 1995, Steve Taneyhill set a new USC record with how many consecutive completed passes?

A. Eleven.

Q. What USC record number of touchdowns was scored against Wichita State University on September 13, 1980?

A. Eight.

Q. After his time at USC F. C. "Buddy" Frick joined what CFL team in 1957?

A. Montreal Alouettes.

Q. USC fans gave what name to the 1920 squad headed by fullback Tatum Wannamaker Gressette?

A. The Wonder Eleven.

Q. Which two members of the 1931 Gamecocks lineup were selected as members of the All-South Atlantic All-Star Team?

A. Earl Clary and Bryant Adair.

───────── 🏈 ─────────

Q. Who did South Carolina play in the inaugural Gator Bowl on January 1, 1946?

A. Wake Forest.

───────── 🏈 ─────────

Q. South Carolina set a school record by scoring how many points against Welsh Neck on October 6, 1903?

A. Eighty-nine.

───────── 🏈 ─────────

Q. What school did the Gamecocks defeat 22–6 in the inaugural game at Columbia's new 18,000-seat Municipal Stadium in 1934?

A. Virginia Military Institute.

───────── 🏈 ─────────

Q. In 1929 who became the first Gamecock to be named All-Southern Conference?

A. Julian Beall.

───────── 🏈 ─────────

Q. Considered by many to be an astronomical amount, for what annual salary did Rex Enright sign a four-year contract with USC in 1938?

A. $5,500.

───────── 🏈 ─────────

Q. Just before graduating from USC, what Gamecock gridiron great died in an car accident near Aiken, South Carolina, on May 10, 1951?

A. Steve Wadiak.

Q. Following his time at USC, halfback Billy Gambrell signed as a free agent with what NFL team?

A. St. Louis Cardinals.

Q. John LaTorre, who captained the Gamecocks for the 1952 season, was known by what nickname?

A. "The Lip."

Q. At 5'7", weighing 155 pounds, what diminutive Gamecock from Hartsville played with a four-year scholarship during the 1950s?

A. Buddy Morrell.

Q. How many yards were the Gamecocks penalized during their 1982 matchup with Richmond?

A. 231.

Q. The Gamecocks played against what team in the 1952 Oyster Bowl at Norfolk, Virginia?

A. Virginia Cavaliers.

Q. In the closing minutes of the 1952 Oyster Bowl with USC trailing fourteen points, how many touchdowns were completed by the Gamecocks within three minutes to clinch the game?

A. Three.

Q. Which USC head football coach was known for his "three yards and a cloud of dust" offense?

A. Warren Giese.

Q. Including two bowl games, what was the average per game rushing yardage for George Rogers during his 1977–80 USC career?

A. 110.7 yards.

———— 🏈 ————

Q. How may seasons did Rex Enright serve as head football coach at USC?

A. Fifteen.

———— 🏈 ————

Q. The 1956 first string became known by what title?

A. "The White Cloud."

———— 🏈 ————

Q. In 1995 Steve Taneyhill set a new USC school record with how many total offensive yards?

A. 3,056.

———— 🏈 ————

Q. What popular South Carolina assistant coach, and later head coach, was known as "The Moose"?

A. Marvin Crosby Bass.

———— 🏈 ————

Q. Early 1960s USC quarterback Jim Costen often entertained teammates by impersonating what then-popular Hollywood actor?

A. James Dean.

———— 🏈 ————

Q. During his USC career (1986–89, including two bowl games) how many of Todd Ellis' 1,350 attempted passes were completed?

A. 747 (55 percent).

Q. During the September 4, 1982, game with Pacific, what Gamecock grabbed a fumble and ran the ball 101 yards for a touchdown?

A. Harry Skipper.

Q. During the October 8, 1994, game with East Carolina, USC set a school record with how many attempted passes?

A. Sixty-one.

Q. "Deacon Dan" was the nickname of what member of the Gamecocks?

A. Daniel Edward Reeves (1962–64).

Q. During the 1971 matchup with North Carolina State, what Gamecock kicker nailed a 52-yard field goal?

A. Tommy Bell.

Q. What Gamecock junior, during the 1971 season, set a NCAA record for most kickoff return yardage with 880 yards?

A. Dickie Harris.

Q. The end of the 1971 season found USC no longer affiliated with what athletic conference?

A. Atlantic Coast Conference (ACC).

Q. How many seasons did Paul Dietzel serve as head football coach at South Carolina?

A. Nine seasons (1966–74).

Q. Who accepted the position of head football coach at USC on December 13, 1974?

A. Jim Carlen.

———— 🏈 ————

Q. Where did Lou Holtz serve as head coach for nine years prior to announcing his move to USC on December 4, 1998?

A. Notre Dame.

———— 🏈 ————

Q. Which South Carolina head coach was known as "Tricky Billy"?

A. William L. "Billy" Laval.

———— 🏈 ————

Q. Gamecock Zola Davis set a USC one game record with how many receptions in the 1998 matchup with Vanderbilt?

A. Fourteen.

———— 🏈 ————

Q. To attend the 1921 matchup with Furman in Greenville, how much did USC fans have to pay for a round-trip train ticket from Columbia and admission to the game?

A. $4.78.

———— 🏈 ————

Q. What Gamecock became mayor of Greenwood, South Carolina?

A. Bill Wohrman.

———— 🏈 ————

Q. What 1904 Gamecock team captain played an entire game against Georgia with a broken jaw?

A. Gene Oliver.

Q. Where did William L. "Billy" Laval coach just prior to joining USC a few days before Christmas 1927?

A. Furman.

Q. What USC gridiron star was known as "The Galloping Ghost from Gaffney"?

A. Earl Clary.

Q. USC Coach Lou Holtz was a lineman at what university?

A. Kent State University.

Q. What early 1980s Gamecock later became a professional wrestler with the WWF?

A. Del Wilkes.

Q. What year did USC have a perfect 3–0 season?

A. 1907.

Q. USC secured its first bowl victory by defeating what team 24–21 in the Carquest Bowl on January 2, 1995?

A. West Virginia.

Q. Though aired only over a local Milwaukee station, who did USC play in its first-ever televised football game on November 5, 1949?

A. Marquette.

Q. During which decade did the Gamecocks have the exact same number of wins as loses?

A. 1930–39 (49–49–7).

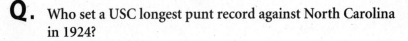

Q. Who coached USC's 1907 football team?

A. Douglas McKay.

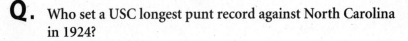

Q. What season did J. P. Moran serve as head coach of the Gamecocks?

A. 1943.

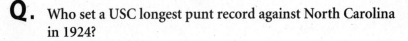

Q. Having racked up 277 total tackles during his three-year career at USC, what Gamecock received All-American honors by the American Football Coaches Association for 1972?

A. John LeHeup.

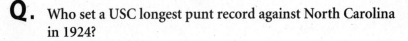

Q. Prior to becoming head football coach at USC, Joe Morrison played for what NFL team from 1959 to 1972?

A. New York Giants.

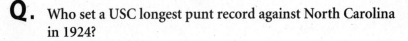

Q. In the 1973 contest with Georgia Tech, USC's Mel Baxley ran the pigskin how many yards to score on a touchdown interception return?

A. 102.

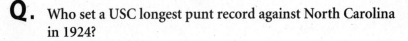

Q. Who set a USC longest punt record against North Carolina in 1924?

A. Bill Jeffords (ninety yards).

Q. Setting a record in the matchup with Mississippi State on October 14, 1995, how many USC passes were completed?

A. Forty.

———— 🏈 ————

Q. In 1972 what underground-type newspaper was pushing for the removal of Paul Dietzel as head football coach at USC?

A. *G.R.O.D.* (Get Rid of Dietzel).

———— 🏈 ————

Q. During the 1973 season Jeff Grantz broke Steve Wadiak's USC record for most yards rushing in a single game with how many yards against Ohio University?

A. 260.

———— 🏈 ————

Q. What 1902–03 football coach at South Carolina later served three seasons as coach at Clemson?

A. C. R. "Bob" Williams.

———— 🏈 ————

Q. Who replaced Rex Enright as head football coach at USC in 1956?

A. Warren Giese.

———— 🏈 ————

Q. Bowing to public outcry over the roughness of the game, what agency abolished football at USC for the 1906 season and half of the 1907 season?

A. University of South Carolina Board of Trustees.

TENNESSEE

CHAPTER ELEVEN

In 1788 North Carolina gave its land holding west of the Great Smoky Mountains to the federal government. These lands comprised the Tennessee region and were designated by the U. S. government as the Territory of the United States South of the River Ohio. Knoxville was made the territorial capital, and on September 10, 1794, the territorial legislature chartered Blount College. The college would struggle for the next thirteen years. On June 1, 1796, Tennessee became the sixteenth state in the Union. In 1807 the fledgling school received a new name: East Tennessee College. The campus consisted of a single building located in what is now downtown Knoxville. In 1809 the school's president, Samuel Carrick, died and the institution was closed. The college reopened in 1820 and construction was started on a new facility on "the Hill." In 1840 two major structures were added to the campus, and the legislature elevated the title of the school from college to university.

East Tennesse University's enrollment was decimated by the Civil War. Students left classes to join both the Union and Confederate armies. Likewise, during the conflict both Union and Confederate forces occupied the campus at different times, and both sides used the university's buildings as hospital facilities. The university grounds suffered from shelling. In 1865 the university reopened with a Union sympathizer as president, which proved of worth in acquiring some $18,500 in restitution funds from the federal government for war damages.

In 1879 the state legislature renamed East Tennessee University, the University of Tennessee (UT), and the rest is history. UT has grown into an academic powerhouse that is recognized not only nationally but also internationally.

Neyland Stadium

Courtesy of University of Tennessee Athletic Department

Q. In what year did the Vols first take to the field in orange jerseys?

A. 1922.

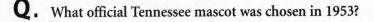

Q. During the 1983–84 seasons, what All-American running back became Tennessee's all-time rushing leader?

A. Johnnie Jones.

Q. What student was responsible for maintaining football on campus in 1894 when there was no official team?

A. William B. Stokely.

Q. Who was the first black athlete to receive a football scholarship at Tennessee?

A. Lester McClain.

Q. Who was the first Vol selected to first-team All-American honors?

A. Gene McEver (1929).

Q. What official Tennessee mascot was chosen in 1953?

A. Smokey, a blue tick coon hound.

Q. In what bowl did Tennessee first play on January 2, 1939?

A. Orange Bowl.

TENNESSEE

Q. What Vol was the 1982 first-round draft pick of the Kansas City Chiefs?

A. Anthony Hancock.

Q. Dean N. W. Dougherty called the firing of what Vol football coach "the best move I ever made"?

A. General Robert R. Neyland.

Q. The Outland Trophy for outstanding lineman in the nation went to what Vol All-American in 1964?

A. Steve DeLong.

Q. Who were the victims of a fourth-quarter rally by Tennessee in the 1988 Peach Bowl?

A. Indiana Hoosiers.

Q. Duke handed Tennessee its greatest ever one-sided defeat, posting what final score?

A. 70–0 (1893).

Q. What Tennessee coach became the youngest head coach in the nation when he was hired at age 28 in 1970?

A. Bill Battle.

Q. By what name is the Tennessee marching band known?

A. Pride of the Southland Band.

TENNESSEE

Q. In what 1971 bowl did Tennessee score 24 points in one quarter?

A. Sugar Bowl.

Q. The NCAA Silver Anniversary Award went to what 1950–52 Vol fullback in 1977?

A. Andy Kozar.

Q. What Vol ended his 1982–85 Tennessee career with 123 receptions?

A. Tim McGee.

Q. At the end of the 1955 season what Vol tailback joined Hank Lauricella and Jimmy Wade as Tennessee's 1,000-yard performers?

A. Johnny Majors.

Q. Vol Curt Watson became a member of what precision Navy flying team in 1982?

A. The Blue Angels.

Q. What early twentieth-century Tennessee four-sport letterman later became nationally known as an outdoorsman, writer, and conservationist?

A. Theophilus Nash Buckingham.

Q. The Vols thrashed Miami in the 1986 Sugar Bowl by what final score?

A. 35–7.

Q. Which Vol, during his 1995–98 career at UT, became the SEC's all-time leading scorer with a total of 371 points?

A. Jeff Hall.

Q. What Tennessee coach inaugurated spring training prior to the 1925 season?

A. M. Beal Banks.

Q. Against what school did Tennessee play to a 10–6 victory in its first homecoming?

A. Vanderbilt.

Q. What was Alan Cockrell's total career passing yardage at Tennessee?

A. 3,823 yards.

Q. In what year did Tennessee's football team adopt the nickname "Volunteers"?

A. 1905.

Q. During the 1951 season, Hank Lauricella set a new Vols single season rushing record with how many yards?

A. 881.

Q. At the 1987 Kickoff Classic game in East Rutherford, New Jersey, what Vol outside linebacker intercepted an Iowa pitchout and ran 96 yards for a touchdown?

A. Darrin Miller.

Q. How many Vol head coaches have served only one year?

A. Five: George Kelley, S. D. Crawford, Andrew Stone, W. H. Britton, and Jim McDonald.

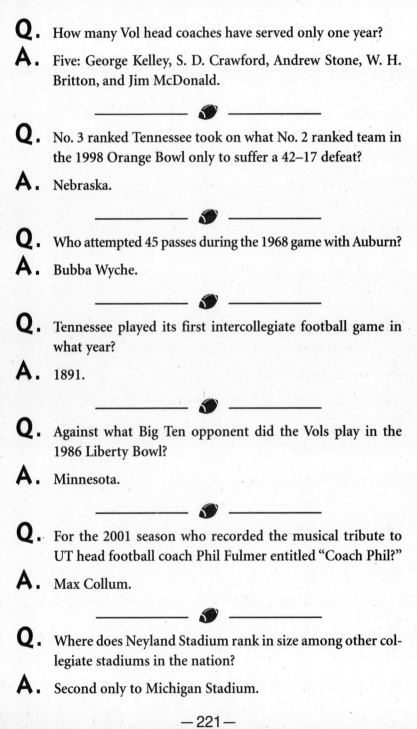

Q. No. 3 ranked Tennessee took on what No. 2 ranked team in the 1998 Orange Bowl only to suffer a 42–17 defeat?

A. Nebraska.

Q. Who attempted 45 passes during the 1968 game with Auburn?

A. Bubba Wyche.

Q. Tennessee played its first intercollegiate football game in what year?

A. 1891.

Q. Against what Big Ten opponent did the Vols play in the 1986 Liberty Bowl?

A. Minnesota.

Q. For the 2001 season who recorded the musical tribute to UT head football coach Phil Fulmer entitled "Coach Phil?"

A. Max Collum.

Q. Where does Neyland Stadium rank in size among other collegiate stadiums in the nation?

A. Second only to Michigan Stadium.

TENNESSEE

Q. How many spectators came to see the first Tennessee football game in Chattanooga?

A. Approximately 100.

Q. What Vol was selected Most Outstanding Player of the 1986 Sugar Bowl?

A. Daryl Dickey.

Q. Who led the Vols in rushing in 1954?

A. Tom Tracey (794 yards).

Q. What team captain was largely responsible for Tennessee changing to orange jerseys with white letters?

A. Roy "Pap" Striegel.

Q. What Tennessee All-American guard played in the 1952 Senior Bowl?

A. Ted Daffer.

Q. In 1933 Tennessee suffered its first shutout for Coach Neyland in 78 games at the hands of what school?

A. LSU (7–0).

Q. The 1968 SEC rushing title went to what Tennessee fullback?

A. Richard Pickens (736 yards).

TENNESSEE

Q. Who was hired as Tennessee's first salaried assistant coach in 1913?

A. Miller "Brute" Pontius.

———————— 🏈 ————————

Q. What two true freshmen earned varsity letters in 1985?

A. Kevin Simons and Keith DeLong.

———————— 🏈 ————————

Q. At the conclusion of its 100-year anniversary season, Tennessee defeated what school 23–22 on January 1, 1991, in the Sugar Bowl?

A. Virginia.

———————— 🏈 ————————

Q. In what bowl did Tennessee play in 1940 and 1945?

A. Rose Bowl.

———————— 🏈 ————————

Q. The Bill Majors Award given for dedication to the game was presented to what 1970 back?

A. Tim Priest.

———————— 🏈 ————————

Q. In what year did Tennessee and Vanderbilt first play each other?

A. 1892.

———————— 🏈 ————————

Q. What two years did Tennessee enjoy back-to-back victories in the Citrus Bowl?

A. 1996 and 1997.

Q. At what university did Doug Dickey pursue his college football career?

A. The University of Florida.

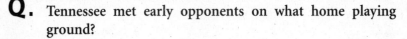

Q. Who scored the only touchdown in the December 16, 1974, Liberty Bowl win over Maryland?

A. Larry Seivers.

Q. Of Peyton Manning's 1,387 attempted passes during his 1994–97 career at UT, how many were completed?

A. 863 (62 percent).

Q. What Vol made a spectacular game-saving interception of an Alabama pass at the line of scrimmage in Tennessee's 16–14 victory in 1985?

A. Dale Jones.

Q. Tennessee met early opponents on what home playing ground?

A. Waite Field.

Q. How many kickoff returns did Willie Gault make during the 1981 season?

A. Twenty-eight.

Q. The *Nashville Banner* named what Tennessee back as the Most Valuable Player in 1939?

A. Bob Foxx.

TENNESSEE

Q. Major Neyland's 1928 Vols rose to national prominence with a 15–13 victory over what opponent?

A. Alabama's Crimson Tide.

———————— 🏈 ————————

Q. Arriving at UT in 1926, what coaches were known as the "Three Musketeers"?

A. Bob Neyland, Paul Parker, and Bill Britton.

———————— 🏈 ————————

Q. In the 1993 Hall of Fame Bowl in Tampa, Tennessee defeated what school 38–23?

A. Boston College.

———————— 🏈 ————————

Q. Who did General Neyland name as the greatest player he ever coached?

A. Gene McEver.

———————— 🏈 ————————

Q. Tennessee met what opponent in its first major bowl contest?

A. Oklahoma (a 17–0 victory in 1939).

———————— 🏈 ————————

Q. Who was the Vols' leading rusher from 1969 to 1971?

A. Curt Watson.

———————— 🏈 ————————

Q. What blocking back received the 1959 and 1960 Jacobs Award?

A. Jim Cartwright.

TENNESSEE

Q. All-American Herman Hickman (1931) played what position?

A. Guard.

———— 🏈 ————

Q. Former Vol Ken Frost played tackle in 1961 and 1962 for what NFL team?

A. Dallas Cowboys.

———— 🏈 ————

Q. During the 1956 game with Vanderbilt, what Vol made a one-handed catch that astounded the players and fans alike?

A. Buddy Cruze.

———— 🏈 ————

Q. Selected to the third team, who became Tennessee's first All-American football player?

A. Graham "Little" Vowell.

———— 🏈 ————

Q. What three Tennessee gridiron stars were named to first-team All-American honors in 1938?

A. Bowden Wyatt, George Cafego, and Bob Suffridge.

———— 🏈 ————

Q. What Vol player completed 29 passes against Florida in 1984?

A. Tony Robinson.

———— 🏈 ————

Q. Tennessee enjoyed its first official undefeated season in what year?

A. 1896.

TENNESSEE

Q. What 1922–1923 Tennessee tackle later became a vice-presidential nominee?

A. Estes Kefauver.

Q. In what year did the Vols not allow a single point to be scored against them during the regular season?

A. 1939.

Q. What Vol tailback won the 1956 Atlanta Touchdown Club Award as the SEC Player-of-the-Year?

A. Johnny Majors.

Q. The Knute Rockne Trophy to the outstanding lineman in college football was presented to what Vol in 1940?

A. Bob Suffridge.

Q. In 1967 what Vol center was selected to the first-team Tennessee Academic All-Americans?

A. Bob Johnson.

Q. When was the first night football game played at Neyland Stadium?

A. September 16, 1972.

Q. Why did the chancellor of Vanderbilt accuse Tennessee of putting too much emphasis on athletics in 1914?

A. Tennessee's 14–7 win over Vanderbilt.

TENNESSEE

Q. What long-time Alabama assistant coach joined the Vol coaching staff in 1985?

A. Ken Donahue.

Q. The low-cut shoe, tearaway jersey, and six-man defensive line were all products of what innovative Vol coach?

A. General Robert R. Neyland.

Q. Tennessee bowed to Iowa, 28–22, in what bowl game?

A. 1982 Peach Bowl.

Q. In the 1972 season finale, what tailback bettered Hank Lauricella's record for single season yardage?

A. Haskel Stanback (890 yards).

Q. Gene McEver earned what descriptive nickname?

A. "The Wild Bull."

Q. When was Phillip "Phil" Fulmer's first season as head football coach at UT?

A. 1992.

Q. Tennessee's first ever victory was over what team?

A. Maryville College.

Q. What Vol was the nation's top punter in 1966, averaging 43.8 yards per kick?

A. Ron Widby.

––––––––––––––––––––––––

Q. Super Turf was installed at Neyland Stadium for the beginning of what season?

A. 1980.

––––––––––––––––––––––––

Q. What 1958 Tennessee tailback was the first Vol in history to complete a pass to himself?

A. Gene Etter (in a game against Ole Miss).

––––––––––––––––––––––––

Q. Tennessee faced what opponent in its first intercollegiate game?

A. Sewanee (1891).

––––––––––––––––––––––––

Q. In what 1994 bowl contest did Tennessee fall victim 31–13 to Penn State?

A. Citrus Bowl.

––––––––––––––––––––––––

Q. Of the five football-playing Majors brothers, how many starred at Tennessee?

A. Three: Johnny, Bill, and Bobby.

––––––––––––––––––––––––

Q. Who led the Vols in passing during the 1977–79 seasons?

A. Jimmy Streater.

Q. How many passes did Steve Alatorre complete in the 1981 Garden State Bowl?

A. Twenty-four.

———————— 🏈 ————————

Q. What Tennessee coach was named National Coach of the Year in 1956?

A. Bowden Wyatt.

———————— 🏈 ————————

Q. What Tennessee triple-threat back was known as the "Hurrying Hungarian"?

A. George Cafego.

———————— 🏈 ————————

Q. Who set Tennessee's record for most punts during a single game in the 1976 game against Kentucky?

A. Craig Colquitt (14 punts).

———————— 🏈 ————————

Q. Tennessee met Emory and Henry on what new home field on September 24, 1921?

A. Shields-Watkins Field.

———————— 🏈 ————————

Q. What Vol center was Tennessee's only selection to the All-SEC team in 1961?

A. Mike Lucci.

———————— 🏈 ————————

Q. During what years did Mickey O'Brien serve as trainer for the Vols?

A. 1938–72.

Q. Who defeated the Vols 42–17 in the 1992 Fiesta Bowl?

A. Penn State.

———— 🏈 ————

Q. How many times did "Bear" Bryant's Kentucky team defeat General Neyland's Vols?

A. None.

———— 🏈 ————

Q. The Vols were ranked number one in the AP and UPI polls before and during what season?

A. 1951.

———— 🏈 ————

Q. What was the final score of the January 2, 1988, Peach Bowl?

A. Tennessee 27–Indiana 22.

———— 🏈 ————

Q. What 1957 Vols tailback first ran the T-formation at Tennessee?

A. Bobby Gordon.

———— 🏈 ————

Q. During the 1949 season J. W. Sherrill set a Tennessee season record with how many pass interceptions?

A. Twelve.

———— 🏈 ————

Q. Who holds the team record for a 100-yard punt made in 1902?

A. A. H. Douglas.

TENNESSEE

Q. What Vol tackle represented Tennessee in the 1981 Japan Bowl?

A. Tim Irwin.

———— 🏈 ————

Q. Tennessee did not field a team in 1898 for what reason?

A. The Spanish-American War.

———— 🏈 ————

Q. Being named to the National Football Foundation and Hall of Fame was an honor bestowed on what former Vol back in 1959?

A. Bobby Dodd.

———— 🏈 ————

Q. Many fans have called what 1956 game "the second greatest college game ever played"?

A. Tennessee's 6–0 win over Georgia Tech.

———— 🏈 ————

Q. On December 30, 1994, Tennessee met and defeated what school 45–23 in the Gator Bowl?

A. Virginia Tech.

———— 🏈 ————

Q. What 1927 Vol team captain later became Tennessee's head football coach?

A. John Barnhill.

———— 🏈 ————

Q. Johnny Majors received All-American honors and finished second in the Heisman Trophy balloting in what year?

A. 1956.

Q. Which 1928 Vols were referred to as Hack, Mack, and Dodd?

A. Buddy Hackman, Gene McEver, and Bobby Dodd.

Q. Against what national champions did the Vols score a 14–13 upset in 1959?

A. LSU.

Q. What years were tagged "the Neyland Era"?

A. 1926–1952.

Q. Tennessee won its first Southern football championship under which head coach?

A. Zora G. Clevenger (1914).

Q. Who led the Vols in punting during 1958 and 1960?

A. Bill Majors.

Q. What 1969 loss knocked previously undefeated Tennessee out of the Top Ten and resulted in the Vols not being invited to play in a major bowl?

A. The 38–0 loss to Ole Miss.

Q. Tennessee met what opponent in the December 20, 1971, Liberty Bowl?

A. Arkansas.

TENNESSEE

Q. The General Robert R. Neyland Trophy was awarded to which individual in 1967 for his contributions to college athletics?

A. Nathan W. Dougherty.

Q. Tennessee's all-time leading scorer Fuad Reveiz set an SEC record for how many consecutive field goals in 1984?

A. Eighteen.

Q. Tennessee coach Bill Battle played his college football at what school?

A. The University of Alabama.

Q. What 1965–67 Vol quarterback was known as "Swamp Rat"?

A. Dewey Warren.

Q. The 2000 Fiesta Bowl saw Tennessee suffer a 31–21 defeat to what midwestern team?

A. Nebraska.

Q. Lettering in 1928, 1929, and 1930, what Vol quarterback only played in one losing game?

A. Bobby Dodd.

Q. What was the name of the 1986 book that detailed the football career of Vols Head Coach Johnny Majors?

A. *You Can Go Home Again.*

TENNESSEE

Q. What 1969–71 Vol place kicker was chosen to the Quarter Century All-SEC team (1950–74) selected in December, 1975?

A. George Hunt.

Q. Who took over head coaching responsibilities at Tennessee following the resignation of General Neyland?

A. Harvey Robinson.

Q. Former Vols Dick Huffman in 1987 and Condredge Holloway in 1999 were elected to what hall of fame?

A. Canadian Football Hall of Fame.

Q. Beattie Feathers played in thirty Tennessee games, scoring how many career touchdowns?

A. Thirty-three.

Q. How many punt returns did Bobby Majors make during 1971?

A. Forty-two.

Q. During his 1981–84 career as a Vol kicker, Jimmy Colquitt averaged how many yards per punt?

A. 43.9.

Q. What 1936–38 lineman later bacame athletic director at Tennessee?

A. Bob Woodruff.

TENNESSEE

Q. What year did Tennessee play its first game with Louisiana-Monroe (formerly Northeast Louisiana)?

A. 2000.

Q. Who kicked the game-winning field goal in the 1957 Gator Bowl?

A. Sammy Burklow.

Q. Doug Dickey left Tennessee with what overall coaching record?

A. 46–15–4.

Q. What Vol was named Most Outstanding Player of the 1971 Sugar Bowl?

A. Bobby Scott.

Q. During his career at Tennessee, 1993–96, Joey Kent had what Vol record number of receptions?

A. 183.

Q. In what year did Johnny Majors assume the head coaching responsibilities at Tennessee?

A. 1977.

VANDERBILT

CHAPTER TWELVE

Cornelius Vanderbilt was born in Staten Island, New York, in 1794. During his lifetime he built an empire based on steamships and railroads. His shipping interests earned him the nickname "Commodore." At the time of his death in 1877, his wealth was estimated in excess of $100 million. Vanderbilt was not known for supporting charities, but his $1 million donation for the founding of a university in a small Tennessee city, which he never visited, made history in education.

In 1872 the Tennessee Legislature had issued a charter for the establishment of Central University in Nashville. A lack of financial resources hampered the opening of the new university in the small city of 40,000. Commodore Vanderbilt's gift enabled the founding of the university to proceed, and in 1873 the proposed Central University was renamed Vanderbilt University. The Commodore put Bishop McTyeire, who had spearheaded the movement for a university in Nashville, in charge of choosing a site for the new campus and to serve as administrator. A stone wall was constructed to keep cows off of the campus, and the first classes opened in October 1875, with 192 students enrolled.

The 323-acre Vanderbilt campus is a national arboretum that features sixty-one species of trees. Vanderbilt University is an independent, privately supported institution, with over 10,000 undergraduates, graduates, and professionals forming the student body. The university is comprised of ten schools of learning that offer degrees in such areas as arts and science, music, law, divinity, philosophy, medicine, nursing, business, and education.

The state-of-the-art VU Medical Center features a Level I Trauma Unit, the NCI designated Vanderbilt-Ingram Cancer Center, a Level I Burn Center, LifeFlight emergency air transport, Voice Center, and the extensive and nationally recognized Children's Hospital.

Vanderbilt Stadium

Courtesy of Vanderbilt University Media Relations Office

VANDERBILT

Q. When did Vanderbilt play its first intercollegiate football game?

A. Thanksgiving Day, November 27, 1890.

———— 🏈 ————

Q. What was former Vandy head football coach Bill Pace's alma mater?

A. Wichita State University.

———— 🏈 ————

Q. How many touchdown passes did Bill Wade throw in the 1950 game with Auburn?

A. Five.

———— 🏈 ————

Q. Who was the captain of the 1953 Commodores?

A. Larry Stone.

———— 🏈 ————

Q. What outstanding Vandy quarterback was killed in a 1917 airplane dogfight over Chateau-Thierry in France?

A. Irby Rice "Rabbit" Curry.

———— 🏈 ————

Q. What is the only year Vanderbilt played Texas Tech?

A. 1974.

———— 🏈 ————

Q. Where was Dan McGugin assistant coach prior to coming to Vanderbilt?

A. University of Michigan.

VANDERBILT

Q. What 6'8", 267-pound Commodore was the largest member of the 1986 team?

A. Greg Smith.

Q. What was the cost of installing natural grass in Vanderbilt Stadium in 1999?

A. $1 million.

Q. What two players teamed up to set a Vandy record by completing an 87-yard pass against LSU in 1945?

A. Tom Gray and Bill Fuqua.

Q. What Vandy athlete received the Most Valuable Player award in 1976?

A. Bernard Wilson.

Q. Vanderbilt's notorious guard, John N. Brown, was known by what nickname?

A. "Bull."

Q. What two Vanderbilt players participated in the 1977 Japan Bowl?

A. Martin Cox and Dennis Harrison.

Q. What honor was bestowed on one-time Vandy football coach Henry Thornton by the British Empire?

A. Knighthood.

VANDERBILT

Q. What 1941 Commodore holds the Vandy record for most points scored in a single season?

A. Jack Jenkins (90 points).

Q. What was Kurt Page's total yardage for the 1983 season?

A. 3,034 yards.

Q. In 1998 what NFL team used Vanderbilt Stadium for its home games?

A. Tennessee Oilers (Titans).

Q. Where did Vanderbilt play its first intercollegiate football game?

A. The YMCA Athletic Park in Nashville.

Q. In the last game of the year, what team spoiled Vandy's otherwise undefeated 1932 season?

A. Alabama.

Q. What was Vanderbilt's record for the magnificent 1904 season?

A. 9–0.

Q. Zealand Thigpen was Vanderbilt's representative at what 1948 All-Star game?

A. The North-South Shrine game.

Q. The Commodores' David Adams is the son of what great Ole Miss All-American fullback?

A. Billy Ray Adams.

Q. Who was the honored guest at the formal dedication of Dudley Field on October 10, 1922?

A. Cornelius Vanderbilt Jr.

Q. Prior to his 1935–39 stint as head football coach, in what other season did Ray Morrison coach the Vandy team?

A. 1918.

Q. What three seasons did Preston Brown lead the Commodores in kick returns?

A. 1976, 1977, and 1979.

Q. In 1897 the City of Nashville notified Vanderbilt that the police had been instructed to stop what post-game activities within city limits?

A. College yells and other post-game noise.

Q. In what year did Vanderbilt last play Yale?

A. 1948.

Q. When did Dan McGugin arrive at Vanderbilt as head football coach?

A. September 17, 1904.

Q. Who dazzled the Vandy fans in 1966 with a 98-yard pass interception return for a touchdown against Citadel?

A. John Gamble.

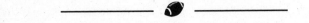

Q. What two brothers played on the 1890 Vandy team?

A. Richard "Rip" Allen and Alex Allen.

Q. In what year did nine Commodores receive All-Southern honors?

A. 1905.

Q. What two Commodores hold the Vandy single-season record for most punts with 79 each?

A. Jerry Shuford (1965) and Alex MacLean (1966).

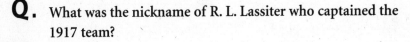

Q. Against what team did Vanderbilt score a 40–0 win in its first intercollegiate football game?

A. University of Nashville (Peabody Normal College).

Q. What was the nickname of R. L. Lassiter who captained the 1917 team?

A. "Big 'Un."

Q. How many years did Red Sanders serve as head football coach at Vanderbilt?

A. Six: 1940–42 and 1946–48.

Q. What team did Vanderbilt play to a scoreless tie at the inaugural game of Dudley Field on October 14, 1922?

A. Michigan.

Q. The 4–0 win over what team proved to be the highlight game of Vandy's 1906 season?

A. Carlisle Indians.

Q. What school defeated the Commodores 83–0 in 1917?

A. Georgia Tech.

Q. In what year was a Jumbotron video screen installed in Vanderbilt Stadium?

A. 1998.

Q. What two Commodores were selected first-team All-SEC in 1941?

A. Bob Gude and Jack Jenkins.

Q. Who captained the 1936 Commodore football team?

A. Herbert G. Plasman.

Q. What seasons did the great quarterback Irby Rice "Rabbit" Curry play at Vanderbilt?

A. 1913–16.

VANDERBILT

Q. In 1987 what Commodore was named the Most Valuable Back in the SEC by the Birmingham Monday Morning Quarterback Club?

A. Eric Jones.

———— 🏈 ————

Q. Who both coached and captained the 1890–92 Vandy football teams?

A. Elliott H. Jones.

———— 🏈 ————

Q. What Vandy tackle ran the famous 1937 "hidden ball" 50 yards for a touchdown against LSU?

A. Greer Ricketson.

———— 🏈 ————

Q. How many penalties did the 1949 Vanderbilt team receive?

A. Seventy-seven.

———— 🏈 ————

Q. In the 1996 matchup with Alabama, what Commodore surprised the Tide by taking a snap from center and running 81 yards for a touchdown?

A. Bill Marinangle.

———— 🏈 ————

Q. What was the only year E. H. Alley was head coach of the Commodores?

A. 1943.

———— 🏈 ————

Q. How many yards did Felix M. Massey race following a fumble to score the winning touchdown against the University of Nashville in 1899?

A. 105.

Q. What Commodore kicked a 55-yard field goal during the 1973 18–16 victory over Tampa?

A. Hawkins Golden.

———— 🏈 ————

Q. What was the weight of the Commodores 1901 quarterback Fred Hume?

A. 122 pounds.

———— 🏈 ————

Q. What two Commodores were selected as Academic All-SEC in 1968?

A. John Burns and Dave Strong.

———— 🏈 ————

Q. Who set a Vandy single season rushing record in 1978?

A. Frank Mordica (1,065 yards).

———— 🏈 ————

Q. In which two seasons were individual game captains selected for the Commodores?

A. 1932 and 1933.

———— 🏈 ————

Q. For what three seasons did Josh Cody receive All-Southern acclaim?

A. 1915, 1916, and 1919.

———— 🏈 ————

Q. What was Head Coach Fred Pancoast's first season with Vanderbilt?

A. 1975.

VANDERBILT

Q. What was the only team to defeat Vanderbilt in 1893?

A. Auburn.

———————— 🏈 ————————

Q. What was the final score of Vanderbilt's first game against Tennessee in 1892?

A. Vanderbilt 22—Tennessee 4.

———————— 🏈 ————————

Q. In 1987 the Commodores set a season record with how many first downs?

A. 237.

———————— 🏈 ————————

Q. How many times was Tom Moore selected first-team All-SEC?

A. Twice: 1958 and 1959.

———————— 🏈 ————————

Q. What former Vanderbilt football team physician was inducted into the Tennessee Sports Hall of Fame in 1985?

A. Dr. Brant Lipscomb.

———————— 🏈 ————————

Q. Who led the Commodores in passing during the 1950 and 1951 seasons?

A. Bill Wade.

———————— 🏈 ————————

Q. From what school did Vanderbilt acquire J. H. Henry as football coach for the 1903 season?

A. University of Chicago.

VANDERBILT

Q. At the invitation of Coach Dan McGugin, what baseball great practiced with the Vandy team one afternoon in the fall of 1911?

A. Ty Cobb.

———— 🏈 ————

Q. In 1999 what Vandy linebacker was named All-American by *Football News*?

A. Jamie Winborn.

———— 🏈 ————

Q. What was the average weight of Vandy's 1891 football team?

A. About 165 pounds.

———— 🏈 ————

Q. How many receptions did Vanderbilt's Keith Edwards make during the 1983 season?

A. Ninety-seven.

———— 🏈 ————

Q. Who was the recipient of Vanderbilt's Wade-Looney Memorial Award for 1963?

A. Bill Waldrup.

———— 🏈 ————

Q. How many players with the last name Brown were on the 1910 Vandy squad?

A. Five: Allen, Bob, Charlie, "Nuck," and Tom.

———— 🏈 ————

Q. What two Commodores share the record of eight interceptions in a single season?

A. Scott Wingfield (1973) and Leonard Coleman (1982).

VANDERBILT

Q. At a sum of $400 per year, who in 1894 became the first salaried football coach at Vanderbilt?

A. Henry Thornton.

———————— 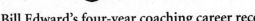 ————————

Q. How many punts did Jim Arnold make during his 1979–82 career at Vanderbilt?

A. 277.

———————— 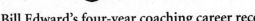 ————————

Q. What inscription was engraved on gold cuff links presented to 1910 team members by the Vanderbilt Athletic Association to commemorate the season's game with Yale?

A. "0–0."

———————— 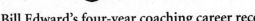 ————————

Q. What position did 1997 All-American Commodore Jamie Robert Duncan play?

A. Linebacker.

———————— 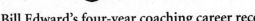 ————————

Q. What are the Vandy colors?

A. Black and gold.

———————— 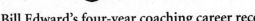 ————————

Q. Out of 1,016 attempts how many passes did Whit Taylor complete during his career at Vanderbilt?

A. 555 (54.6 percent).

———————— 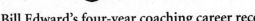 ————————

Q. What was Bill Edward's four-year coaching career record at Vanderbilt?

A. 21–19–2.

VANDERBILT

Q. Which Commodore in 1996 ran a 96-yard kickoff return for a touchdown against Kentucky?

A. Jimmy Williams.

———— 🏈 ————

Q. What Commodore scored 25 touchdowns during his 1947–50 career at Vanderbilt?

A. Dean Davidson.

———— 🏈 ————

Q. Who was the first Vandy player to be selected All-Southern?

A. John J. Tigert (1903).

———— 🏈 ————

Q. Against what team did Vandy's Ricky Anderson kick an 82-yard punt in 1984?

A. Georgia.

———— 🏈 ————

Q. Who in 1921 became the first son to follow in his father's footsteps as a Vandy football player?

A. Frank A. Godchaux Jr.

———— 🏈 ————

Q. What three brothers played on the Vandy football team in 1906?

A. Bob, Dan, and Vaughn Blake.

———— 🏈 ————

Q. Who set a Vanderbilt scoring record during his 1981–84 career as a Commodore?

A. Ricky Anderson (192 points).

VANDERBILT

Q. In what year was the Old Dudley Field, later called Curry Field, opened for play?

A. 1892.

Q. Who quarterbacked the memorable 1969 14–10 Vandy upset of Alabama?

A. Watson Brown.

Q. What famous question originated from the 1896 fight between Vanderbilt and University of Nashville players?

A. "Who hit Looney?"

Q. Jim Popp, Steve Wade, and Will Wolford all shared what SEC honor in 1985?

A. First-team All-SEC.

Q. The 1907 matchup between Vanderbilt and Michigan in Nashville set a Southern football attendance record with how many spectators?

A. Approximately nine thousand.

Q. What seasons did Steve Sloan head the Commodores as coach?

A. 1973 and 1974.

Q. With a total of 41 passes during 1979–82, who set a Vandy record for most career touchdown passes?

A. Whit Taylor.

Q. During what two years did Vandy's Ken Cooper play with the Baltimore Colts?

A. 1949 and 1950.

———— 🏈 ————

Q. How many points did Vanderbilt score, leading the nation in scoring for the first three games, in the 1912 season?

A. 305.

———— 🏈 ————

Q. What Commodore punted for 74 yards in the 1960 game against Kentucky?

A. Hank Lesesne.

———— 🏈 ————

Q. Which successful coach began his coaching career as assistant to Dan McGugin in 1921 and 1922?

A. Wallace Wade.

———— 🏈 ————

Q. In what year was Vanderbilt's William D. "Billy" Spears inducted into the National Football Hall of Fame?

A. 1962.

———— 🏈 ————

Q. Vanderbilt became a charter member of what conference in 1893?

A. Southern Intercollegiate Athletic Association.

———— 🏈 ————

Q. Who was the first American Indian to play on the Vanderbilt football team?

A. J. B. McAlester (1897 and 1898).

Q. Who in 1935 became Vanderbilt's first player to receive first-team All-SEC honors?

A. Charles Francis "Willie" Geny.

————  ————

Q. What seasons did Watson Brown serve as head football coach at Vanderbilt?

A. 1986–90.

————  ————

Q. Commodore Will Wolford was a first-round draft choice of what NFL team in 1986?

A. Buffalo Bills.

————  ————

Q. How many punts were returned by the Commodores in 1948?

A. Fifty-five.

————  ————

Q. What five-year-old served as the Commodore mascot in 1905?

A. Bob McNeilly.

————  ————

Q. During the 1930 game with Ole Miss, what Commodore scored touchdown runs of 63, 61, and 19 yards?

A. Amos "Mouse" Leonard.

————  ————

Q. What honor did Vanderbilt coach George MacIntyre receive from the *Sporting News* in 1982?

A. National Coach of the Year.

VANDERBILT

Q. Before becoming head football coach at Vanderbilt on December 5, 1985, where did Watson Brown coach the previous two years?

A. Rice University.

———————— 🏈 ————————

Q. What was the final score in Vanderbilt's lopsided victory over Bethel College in 1912?

A. 105–0.

———————— 🏈 ————————

Q. Boyce Smith (against Florida in 1958) and John Schaffler (against Louisville in 1971) hold the Vandy record for how many punts in one game?

A. Fourteen.

———————— 🏈 ————————

Q. How many times did Vandy fumble the ball in 1979?

A. Forty-one.

———————— 🏈 ————————

Q. Vanderbilt played two games each with what two schools in 1891?

A. Sewanee and Washington University.

———————— 🏈 ————————

Q. With what Canadian Football League team did Commodore George Deiderich sign in 1960?

A. Montreal Alouettes.

———————— 🏈 ————————

Q. What Vandy player made Academic All-American two years in a row?

A. Doug Martin (1973 and 1974).

Q. Against what opponent did Watson Brown coach in the 1986 and 1987 Tulane games?

A. Mack Brown, his younger brother.

———— 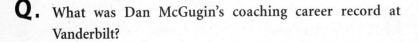 ————

Q. What Vanderbilt fullback led the nation in scoring in 1927?

A. Jimmy Armistead (138 points).

————

Q. In 1997 who became the head football coach at Vandy?

A. Woody Widenhofer.

————

Q. What was Ricky Anderson's career punting yardage average?

A. 45.6 yards per punt.

————

Q. What Commodore played for the New York Giants in 1925 and 1926?

A. Lynn Bomar.

————

Q. What was Dan McGugin's coaching career record at Vanderbilt?

A. 197–55–19.

————

Q. With what professional team did Allama Matthews sign after completing his career at Vanderbilt?

A. Atlanta Falcons.

VANDERBILT

Q. What newspaper writer and former Vanderbilt quarterback first applied the name *Commodores* to the Vanderbilt football team in 1897?

A. William E. Beard of the *Nashville Banner*.

———— 🏈 ————

Q. How many kick returns did Lee Nallen make in 1948 and 1949?

A. Forty-three (in both years).

———— 🏈 ————

Q. The Commodores' Bill Wade played with what two NFL teams?

A. Los Angeles Rams and Chicago Bears.

———— 🏈 ————

Q. In Vandy's 1924 6–3–1 season, what team tied the Commodores?

A. Quantico Marines.

———— 🏈 ————

Q. In 1995 who followed Gerry DiNardo as head football coach at Vanderbilt?

A. Rod Dowhower.

———— 🏈 ————

Q. What was the cost of the 1980–81 construction of Vanderbilt Stadium?

A. $10.6 million.

———— 🏈 ————

Q. Who holds the Vandy career record for most points after touchdown?

A. Mike Woodard (80 points).